A Manifesto on Palestine

RETHINKING LIBERATION FROM BELOW

Ibraheem Rasras

Daraja Press

Published by
Daraja Press
https://darajapress.com
Wakefield, Quebec, Canada
2025

ISBN: 9781998309672 (softcover)
ISBN: 9781998309689 (ebook)

Library and Archives Canada Cataloguing in Publication

Title: A manifesto on Palestine : rethinking liberation from below / Ibraheem Rasras.
Names: Rasras, Ibraheem, author.
Description: Includes bibliographical references.
Identifiers: Canadiana (print) 2025023131X | Canadiana (ebook) 20250231352 |
ISBN 9781998309672
   (softcover) | ISBN 9781998309689 (EPUB)
Subjects: LCSH: Palestinian Arabs—Political activity. | LCSH: Government, Resistance to—Palestine.
   LCSH: Arab-Israeli conflict.
Classification: LCC DS119.76 .R37 2025 | DDC 956.9405/5—dc23

It began dreadfully, progressed tragically, creating its own symbol from the mixture of dread and tragedy, and then ended dreadfully. But it recreated a new dreadful beginning from the dread of that end. To legitimize that new, horrific beginning, it utilized the symbol created by that mixture, which remained unending.

Contents

Introduction

Palestine will never achieve freedom without bottom-up resistance. This resistance also requires a bottom-up framework consisting of a) a unified mode of ethics, b) a collective understanding of the leading cause, and c) consistent, regulated practices based on the first two. This claim arises from the recurrence of atrocities reminiscent of the Deir Yassin and Sabra and Shatila massacres, which resurfaced in Gaza in 2023, 2024, and 2025. The devastation, with numerous destroyed blocks that, when seen through a colonial lens, resemble ruins, starkly presents the impact on human lives. The scene of crushed bodies under not only the rubble of those destroyed blocks but also the military trucks and bulldozers, alongside abandoned clothes and shoes, all seem like remnants of an Eastern species, as read through the debris they left behind. These trucks are powerful machines from the late 20th and early 21st centuries, embodying Hegel's description of the end of history, specifically the "absolute knowing," where human knowledge reaches its peak of progression (G. W. Hegel 2018, 454).

Does this absolute knowledge essentialize testing the limits of militarized power on human bodies, emotions, or other expressions of human existence? Could it represent the endpoint of human existence on Earth, guided by the pursuit of producing nuclear weapons and other destructive inventions born from this human knowledge at the end of history? Or could it be that this knowledge is more easily and logically used to make some groups stronger than others, such that the latter serve as victims to the former's absolute knowledge?

These inquiries generally guide the formulation of the central investigation of this book. This central inquiry highlights explicitly three main elements: the position of Palestinians, their condition of civilization, and their misguided path to self-building led by the Palestinian Authority. For the last element, the Oslo Accords serve as an exemplary model, but mainly as a shock to the self-building process that Palestinians were collectively undertaking during the revolution led by the Palestinian Liberation Organization (PLO).

Not only does the Palestinian condition concern the material crisis of occupation, dispossession, and statelessness, but it also entails an epistemological crisis, one in which the structures of liberation have beenw subverted, diverted, or rendered ineffective by the very forces they seek to fight. It is not only about the continuity of Zionist settler-colonialism's brutal existence but also the self-imposed framework of its logic on Palestinian resistance. This self-imposed framework, in turn, is most prominently manifest in the adoption of hierarchical, statist, and, more profoundly, technocratic forms of liberation. These are the forms that resemble the configuration of the oppressor while shedding the ethical, communitarian, and revolutionary forces that once propelled the Palestinian cause. More importantly, the Oslo Accords embody this collapse not only as a failed diplomatic endeavor but also as the moment when resistance transformed into formalized managerial governance and the language of liberation gave way to development, recognition, and conditional sovereignty.

This Manifesto asserts that the Palestinian crisis must be redefined not merely as a lack of international law, diplomacy, and institutional politics but rather as a void in the political context and ethical framework of the ruling political system, as manifested in both Gaza and the West Bank. On this basis, this core problem is seen as worsened by types of violence (i.e., symbolic and physical) perpetrated through distorted views of Palestine within many societies that treat Palestinians as either subhuman or terrorists, neglecting their role in fighting for agency, willingness to self-determination, and their struggle for justice. Palestine is considered a victim of dominant power control visions that strategically erase its existence. Addressing this profound issue requires resistance not only politically and materially but also with transformative decolonial authority—one that counters the colonial structure of the framework within which Palestine is studied, disseminated, and endorsed.

Problem Statement

The Palestinian liberation struggle has, over the past decades, been imagined within factional, hierarchical, and reactionary paradigms replete with colonial and neoliberal rhetoric. Palestinian forms of resistance have, over the years, evolved from revolutionary bottom-up rhetoric to institutionalized, formalized, and eventually compromised modes of governance and resistance, particularly in the wake of the Oslo Accords. While material dispossession, military occupation, and state violence are apparent axes of Palestinian suffering, a no less urgent yet unaddressed issue is that of the epistemological crisis on the Palestinian self-ruling level. This crisis consists of the endorsement of the oppressor's paradigms, de-legitimation of values of liberation, and the inability to construct a standard, dynamic, and bottom-up resistance based on Palestinians' everyday lives and cultural habits. In brief, the underlying problem that this Manifesto seeks to address is the struggle of the Palestinian resistance to develop a political imagination and resistance framing[1], reclaiming resistance on an embodied, ethical, anarchic, and decolonial axis.

Research Questions

1. How can Palestinian resistance be conceptualized beyond factional, hierarchical, and technocratic imaginaries and instead employ an anarchistic and decolonial logic?

2. What are the epistemological and historical origins of the contemporary obstacles of Palestinian resistance tactics, namely, on the local level in the post-Oslo Accords?

3. How do everyday life, grassroots networks, and popular struggles lay the basis for modern ethics of resistance?

4. How can the current claim of self-determination in Palestine be examined through critical theory, anarchist anthropology, psychoanalysis, and decolonial thought?

5. From what expansive ethical position can Palestinian colonial rule and internal authoritarianism be opposed and resisted within Palestinian political life?

The Oslo Accords were an attempt at an agreement between Fatah and Israel aimed at reconciliation. They are sometimes compared

---

1 For example, the Palestinian Authority claims to be part of the Palestinian national project and to follow a strategy of peaceful popular resistance. However, in reality, its strategy is full of opportunism, exploitation, and other unethical elements. This challenges the very concept of resistance, particularly the peaceful form we have encountered in other forms of resistance, such as Gandhi's Salt March, given that the Palestinian Authority considers itself a model emulating Gandhi's project.

to other pacts or agreements, such as those conducted in Northern Ireland and Algeria, which paved the way for French withdrawal, or the American withdrawal from Vietnam, among others (Lustick 1997, 61). In the Accords, Fatah, represented by Arafat, recognized for the first time Israel and the Israeli right to exist within the Palestinian territories (Shlaim 1994, 62). The Accords have reshaped the "Israeli-Palestinian, Israeli-Jordanian, Israeli-Syrian, and Israeli-Lebanese" relations.

On the one hand, they did not bring about a significant historical transformation in the lives of Palestinians.

On the other hand, the Accords benefited Israelis and allowed them to expropriate more land and achieve greater control over Palestinian territories. However, overall, the Accords failed to achieve the expected outcomes, and, as Shlaim argues (ibid.), their failure demonstrates how the Palestinian case is fundamentally different from other experiences in Northern Ireland, Algeria, Vietnam, and so on.

More than three decades have passed, and Palestinians have been unable to develop a solid attitude in facing Israeli plans. On this basis, the Accords are viewed here as a crisis that must be comprehended not only within the practice but also on a perceptual level. Eventually, one must wonder: what should the alternative be to stop the Palestinians' suffering?

Resistance, in the Palestinian case, should grow like a tree that feeds on the already existing sources and resources surrounding and accessible to it. In the same way, Palestinian resistance should draw from the already existing phenomena of resistance that people practice in their daily lives, often without noticing them and, thus, without planning to systematize them.

The analysis is not limited to the political realm but also encompasses cultural, sociological, and psychological contexts, as well as urban design in post-Oslo Palestine. This inquiry aims to develop a new roadmap that generates new insights into Palestine and the Palestinian Cause, including perspectives rooted in the lived experiences of Palestinians. The analysis provides a brief examination of some historical events in Palestine's history, Israeli policies and actions, the general urban design in the occupied Palestinian territories, the social systems in place, and, last but not least, the political economy of the Palestinian

Cause. By correlating different schools of thought or mainstreams, this Manifesto seeks to produce a new critical intellectual perspective.

The aim here is to provide insights into and understandings of concepts that are deeply essential yet often absent or distorted in the Palestinian case, such as power, resistance, liberation, and freedom. By drawing on ideas and perspectives from scholars of critical theory, anarchism, and other schools of thought, the aim is to provide fresh insights into the Palestinian case. These insights may be classified as radical critiques of Zionist imperialism as well as of Palestinian daily life, the forms of subjection faced by Palestinians, and the politically distorted practices of Hamas and Fatah. These insights also draw from philosophers and scholars who failed to warn the world about Zionism's growing impacts despite recognizing them—Marcuse, Arendt, and Levinas. Above all, the core aim remains to expose the falsification behind the ordinary misrepresentation of concepts (e.g., freedom and resistance) made by many Palestinian figures or groups.

Lastly, it is termed a Manifesto for several reasons. First, it suggests a direct form of communication with Palestinians and pro-Palestinians, who are ready to support Palestinians in achieving their liberation and self-building. Second, it serves as a testament to the various failed strategies and attempts Palestinians have made to change their circumstances, such as the "Unity Government Formation" that took place in 2014 (*U.N. chief welcomes the formation of a Palestinian unity government*, 2014), which, as seen in 2024, ultimately failed. Ultimately, the goal is to provide an urgent alternative program to guide Palestinians in devising a new strategy based on research into both the perceptual level and the possible set of practices for resistance and freedom construction in Palestine. Based on an investigation of several approaches and theories from multiple schools of thought and groups, this Manifesto proposes a new understanding of the crucial practices of resistance and freedom in Palestine, aiming to strengthen new pathways that align with a renewed Palestinian civilization and an independent, collective self-reflection.

A Perception of Reformulating Resistance, Freedom, and the Process of Self-Building

The design of understanding informs the writing process by addressing errors in resistance, freedom, and self-building in both perception and practice. These errors encourage consideration of how each error exists within its domain, as discussed in the Manifesto. First, it is essential to acknowledge that resistance, although prevalent in the Palestinian context, lacks diversity in its methods, particularly in everyday life activities such as commuting or agricultural work. Second, freedom should be understood as multi-dimensional since it encompasses both daily routines and the political practices of the Palestinian Authority (PA). Third, self-building emerges as the next stage, following the resolution of issues related to freedom and resistance, to create a new civilization aligned with the liberation process and future nation-building efforts. Lastly, these critiques and insights should be paired with an understanding of how other nations have liberated themselves and built their own identities.

According to Bourdieu, lacking a "'self-regulating market,' educational system, juridical apparatus, and State" (Bourdieu 2013, 183) results in relations of power less stable, less perpetuated, and less consistent. Although the Palestinian context has its particularities, these are indeed relevant to how Palestinians, lacking precise construction and systematization, have developed their education, judiciary, and a distorted semi-statehood system, which lacks a stable and consistent regulatory mechanism and an independent economic system. This deficiency is reflected in the rationalization of Palestinian daily life.

To be realistic, resistance must surprise the aggressor by exceeding expectations, taking into account the knowledge of the tools used to suppress resistance. Otherwise, resistance will be consistently contained and will not stray from the orbit the aggressor already knows well or perhaps even created for the colonized or the oppressed. In the simplest demonstration, resistance should be shocking to the aggressor! That requires a historical knowledge of what can be integrated into the resistance as a whole, combining the tenacity, ingenuity, and resourcefulness of the colonized.

Additionally, it is imperative to grasp the political economy of resistance resources and to break with any ultimate dependence on past forms of resistance, thereby protecting resistance as an approach to a free life. The political economy of resistance symbolizes the socio-economic conditions that shape the concept of resistance and the framework within which it operates. For example, in the Palestinian context, it's crucial to investigate how resistance will function in a world where the economy is driven by neoliberalism and its fundamental principles, such as individualism, private interest, and profit-making. Following the Marxist emphasis on the essential role of political economy in structuring the superstructure, ethics are likewise shaped by the political economy governing socioeconomic life. To guide this investigation into ethics, the discussion will shift toward the virtues underlying the normativity of ethics, thereby helping to close the gap in recognizing how practices cultivate virtues or ethics.

The ethics of resistance are to be inspired by the Ethics of Liberation, the Pedagogy of the Oppressed, the idea of freedom according to Hegel,[2] and further sources, including concepts from the psychology of colonialization, the psychology of the occupied people, and the ambiguous containment of the people's refusals of political oppression, historical injustice, and social vulnerability. At first glance, the ethics of resistance seem to relate to a system of ethics that functions as boundaries against unethical practices, such as killing innocents or torturing people. However, this is not its entire narration.

The ethics of resistance sometimes serve as emancipatory codes. At other times, they attempt to present guidelines that orient people toward certain conclusions. Consequently, they are not defined at the outset but emerge as the research process unfolds. What can be said here is that these ethics indicate a regulatory framework that touches upon all practices associated with resistance and all domains of Palestinian daily life (inside Palestine). The ethics of resistance must directly confront neoliberal values, including profit maximization and utilitarian calculations.

---

2 Hegel's perception of freedom is important as he links personality to freedom and perception. So, there is a link between what percepts, internally interprets it, and develops it either into a conception or a practice as outcomes. These outcomes allow that human being to possess personality, which represents that this person enjoys freestanding.

Additionally, they should elaborate on how and why ethics must be integrated into the confrontation of the decades-long daily checkpoints and collective dependency connected to: 1. a feeling of inferiority stemming from class of secondary citizenship; 2. the internalized cultural degradation of the colonized as less civilized; 3. the fear from unjustified killing; and 4. restrictive urban design as seen in geographical segregations closures of, between, or within Palestinians territories.

Several books will be used as references to understand the impact of economics and social systems on shaping or influencing ethics. This ethical framework suits a Manifesto intended to diagnose Palestinian dilemmas and produce critiques and strategies concluded from these critiques against the dilemmas. The ethics of resistance should be presented in the Palestinian context, with an understanding that the Palestinian Cause in a world dominated by neoliberal economics introduces new insights into resistance. To give the concept a new ethos, Deleuze's Difference and Repetition will guide the comprehension of self-creation through repeated practices or ideas. Resistance can also terminologically reflect an opposing stance to dependency, which may be a part of the daily life activities of the oppressed people, who, daily, lose their lands and face humiliation at checkpoints or during raids on their houses and shops. This explanation helps to clarify their case of civilization and how it is not emancipatory.

To explore this matter of civilization and its dependency, considering its inability to serve Palestinian society, the fragility of the Palestinian Authority has been exposed to public opinion, and it faces numerous internal and external calls for necessary internal reforms. What is striking, however, is the clarity of its approach, which defines its failure in governance. For example, its undefined dependence on foreign aid and resources, exposed by its debt crisis, is conclusive evidence of the PA's declining approach. Its continuation will lead to a cultural dependency that prevents local Palestinian society from progressing due to the massive debt and all the associated conditions. In numbers:

In Q1 2024, public debt reached $3.9bn (12.9% increase compared to Q1 2023), most of which is domestic debt (65.5%) to banks and local institutions, as well as some international debt liabilities. Furthermore, the PNA had about $4bn in arrears to the private sector, public servants, and others in Q1 2024, a 25.7% increase compared to Q1 2023. The public debt and arrears totalled $7.9bn in Q1 2024, 45.2% of the Palestinian GDP in 2023, a ratio that is bound to rise close to a critical threshold of 60% as GDP plummets in 2024. Compounding the PNA's financial crisis, budget support has been minimal, amounting to only $84.8mn in Q1 2024 *(Team 2024)*.

While discussing debt, it is essential to consider the ongoing war and its consequences; however, these debt accumulations are not a result of the past two years. Instead, they began accumulating significantly before that due to factors such as corruption and a lack of transparency. Nevertheless, it is essential to understand the accumulation of these debts in light of the Palestinian Authority's preparedness to confront challenges and emergencies, such as wars and disasters, as well as its development and economic plans.

Resistance, in the Palestinian case, also serves as a guiding approach to self-building, certainly when people participate in shaping their future alongside resistant groups. Hence, to avoid collective alienation, ordinary Palestinians must construct their means of self-protection and be aware of their oppressor to act beyond the restrictions that the oppressor may impose.

In the first chapter of the Manifesto, it will be suggested that the ethics of resistance and the need for a cultural revolution are significantly interconnected. Specifically, the ethics of resistance represent a spirit of cultural revolution; these ethics correct the traditional understandings of ethics, resistance, culture, and revolution and reinvent a new trajectory for a revolution that should be seen as cultural. These principles act as facilitators in making the concrete vision of 'ethics of resistance' plausible. The relationship between the ethics of resistance and cultural revolution is rooted in a specific social form of consciousness and epistemology that actively transforms Palestinian reality, such as the ethics of resistance becoming situated as an ethos within society.

Nevertheless, the issue remains: how will this reflection help us grasp the problematic frameworks of civilization and self-constructing?

These are practices, discourses, and ethics that together shape the fabric of Palestinian life. Thus, the different dimensions of human life in Palestine are closely related to all ideas associated with Palestine, particularly the clichés of terrorism claims, conditions of suffering and injustice, revolutionary resistance, and every component that has contributed to or shaped the portrayal of Palestinians over the past 75 years.

Between Political Science, Sociology, Political Psychology, and Anthropology

Psychoanalysis in the Frame of Colonialism and Postcolonialism

The Colonial Mechanisms to Create Space for Itself

The process of training and conditioning one group of people to serve another, often with the latter's consent in exchange for specific considerations, represents a triumph for the latter. These considerations may be financial, unethical, or inhumane; nonetheless, they are realistic and can function as de facto incentives. For example, colonized people might be permitted to use products created by colonizers on colonized lands, utilizing their own resources, such as civil infrastructure or employment opportunities within the colonial administration. These privileges exemplify the logic of colonialism by aligning the interests of the colonized with the broader ambitions of colonial domination. They also reflect the colonizer's belief in its own civilizational superiority or moral heroism. Was this logic not embedded in the United Kingdom's self-designation as "Great" Britain or in the United States' self-image as a global hegemonic power?

In European colonial discourse, the dominance of the self over the other is made explicit. As Ella Shohat argues, Europeans perceived and presented themselves as teachers with nothing to learn from the Afro-Asian populations they colonized (Shohat 2018, 165). Africans and Asians were portrayed as lacking historical experience compared to Europeans, who were deemed to have compelling historical experiences in Asia and Africa. This view rests on assumptions of European racial and cultural purity (ibid., 164).

Reconsidering Levinas's argument, one may conclude that individuals are often forced to choose between two "evils": suppression or chaos (Levinas 1979, 15). Similarly, colonized nations, after prolonged resistance and the imposition of a colonial identity, are left with limited choices, choices predetermined mainly by the colonizers.

Levinas, for instance, contemplates that the way Heidegger presents the "Other" as subordinate to the "being" reflects obedience to the unknown, which, in turn, leads to subjugation to "another power." This power could appear as an imperialist regime or a despotic system (ibid, 46-47).

Another dimension of the relationship between colonialism and psychoanalysis can be understood by observing how colonial powers intentionally created local chaos through various methods, including the "traditional method" that was utilized across different colonial eras. Fanon, when explaining this traditional colonial method, used examples of systematic arrests, spreading propaganda among tribes, and forming parties from the disorganized "lumpenproletariat" (Fanon, *The Wretched of the Earth* 1963, 115). Clearly, by deploying a divide-and-conquer strategy (DCP), colonial regimes designed specific mechanisms to control the entirety of colonized societies.

What remains less clear, however, is the voluntary engagement of some reactionary groups from colonized people with the DCP process. Some chose to collaborate with colonial powers, such as those tribes that embraced colonial propaganda, members of the lumpenproletariat, and local elites, often in the hope of inheriting the power structures left behind by the colonizers, such as security forces or the bureaucratic foundations of a future post-colonial state. These collaborators become implicated in colonial mechanisms, not simply as victims but as agents with aspirations to rule in the colonial regime's image.

The Colonized's Voluntary Adaptation to Colonialism: Reflections and Interactions

Some dynamic factors from the colonial era persisted into the post-colonial period and became dominant in the later period. Homi Bhabha's engagement with this experience led him to ask:

> How do strategies of representation or empowerment come to be formulated in the competing claims of communities where, despite shared histories of deprivation and discrimination, the exchange of values, meanings, and priorities may not always be collaborative and dialogical but may be profoundly antagonistic, conflictual and even incommensurable? *(Bhabha 1994, 2)*.

Addressing this matter in the Palestinian political experience manifests a surface-level oppression occurring in Palestine before and during the war on Gaza, which masks an even deeper, unmarked oppression arising from within. In a simplistic sense, one can imagine the claim through the case of an oppressed, poor, widowed woman on whose behalf a well-dressed, non-elected politician or academic speaks. Once this politician or academic arises as a leader, due to reasons related to the centrality of their place of origin, socioeconomic background, familial privileges, or otherwise, this scene should be viewed within a network of events or societal phenomena, all functioning as a totality that damages the spontaneity of liberation as a practice and trivializes the perception of liberation by rendering it stylistic in an era where the Palestinian Cause struggles.

In this example, 'stylistic' refers to those leaders who visualize their imagined scheme of liberation as the ultimate path to redemption. This perspective helps explain why liberation, as a project, may fail, particularly when these leaders impose their principles on real-life situations instead of adapting them to meet the needs of reality (Lenin 1973). Their projected perceptions are generated at the expense of other, potentially better, and more effective principles. These leaders are defined as alienus leaders because they gain power unpopularly, lack a revolutionary lens, and, as a result, do not enjoy people's allegiance. These alienus leaders establish their unconscious on this basis. They maintain power either through the extreme suppression of those with differing ideologies or because society itself lacks a revolutionary encountering agency.

The concept of stylistics can be better understood by realizing how these leaders establish a relationship between 1. the misrepresentation of liberation in order to maintain power, 2. the misuse of the natural need for leadership in this context, and 3. the systematic, falsified perception of liberation that results from the first two elements. The systematization of this perception, expressing its continuity through later stages, is what makes the matter stylistic. In brief, there is a natural need for both liberation and leadership, and it is the people who need them. Certain circumstances enable leaders to acquire power. These leaders view it as an opportunity to abuse their position and misrepresent the values of liberation and leadership to maintain power.

Another explanation for this is that liberation is pursued by following the tools of trivialization that belong to the current era without considering the specificity or sensitivity related to the praxis of liberation. In the operation of trivialization-making, there are two engaging parties: the creators of the tools of trivialization and those who apply these tools in their own context—usually unconsciously. Those who use these external tools[3] are not involved in their creation, so it is anticipated that they unconsciously provide justification and meaning to the process once they consent to it and begin to use the tools to shape their subjectivity. Once the operation gains justification and the meaning of the trivial act becomes clear, it consequently develops its rationality, allowing the process to continue.

This is particularly relevant when attempting liberation through mechanisms that may be secondary rather than fundamentally radical. In the context of this Manifesto, this claim is, for example, apparent in Fatah's (Hamas and Fatah: How are the two groups different? 2017) approach, which seeks to end the occupation through prolonged peace negotiations, introduced as the only form of liberation. When the secondary is placed in the position of the radical, liberation becomes compromised by the subordination of the secondary: negotiating peace, which should follow liberation, is instead placed before it.

Both meanings of the stylistic, 1. alienus leaders and their imposed principles and 2. the pursuit of liberation through tools of trivialization, contain some form of externalization. More directly, externalization occurs when tools of trivialization are foreign to the collective entity's situation and the realistic conditions of liberation and when these tools do not enhance Palestinian modes of thinking about their own social, economic, and cultural requirements essential to liberation. This is clear in practices such as consumerism, economic openness based on mutual agreements between colonizer and colonized, and the use of excessive violence to achieve liberation, which later transforms into local suppression.

Colonization itself represents an externalizing force that creates a reality imposed upon the colonized people. As a result, the colonized

---

3 Foreign tools here refer to the Western globalized tools that can be associated with the global capitalist system and can be values, institutional procedures, ideologies, or even more. Individualism can be one such tool.

find themselves needing to restore their lands and dismantle the colonial regime along with its post-colonial impacts. Based on this, colonization should be presented as a highly sensitive era in the history of the colonized: one which, if not well-addressed, can become a long-term "obstructive force" in the path of self-building.

Externalization, in the context of colonization, can be viewed as a form of alienation that impedes collective self-control. By 'external' in the colonizing process, it means that colonization begins by establishing a form of sovereign power shaped by its own authority and its particular conception of modern politics. More theoretically, following Butler's illustration of power as an external force exerted against the subject, lowering and subordinating them (Butler 1997, 1-2), one may begin to anatomize the role of this external factor, which seeks to assign a degraded identity to the colonized. But would this not require some internal reasoning to justify that identity? Indeed, it would require internalized incorporation by the colonized. And in many cases, colonization achieved its aims through the unconscious participation of the colonized themselves. Here, it is essential to note the role of violence that the colonized inherit from the colonizer.

Local despotism, factional branching, and sectarian or tribal conflicts are among the many examples in which colonialism succeeded in securing voluntary adaptation to its ambitions of domination. In *Black Skin, White Masks*, Fanon introduces the concept of the "Unconscious" by describing an unintentionally formed "disturbing distance in-between" the "Colonialist Self" and the "Colonized Other" (Fanon, *Black Skin, White Masks* 1986, xvi). Specifically, in the colonized's attempt to differentiate themselves from the colonizers, they end up reflecting the other (i.e., the colonizer) in themselves (i.e., the colonized). Fanon suggests that this reflection happens unconsciously and can even be perceived on the body of the colonized—marked by the remnants of the colonizer (Fanon, *Black Skin, White Masks* 1986).

Lacan's conception of the unconscious plays a deep and fundamental role (Lacan 1998, 39). Inspired by his conception, Žižek connects the unconscious to the future—with all its expectations, details, and shifts (Žižek, *The Sublime Object of Ideology* 1989, 58). In unconscious thinking, the concept of "error" plays a crucial role in determining how "truth" becomes perceived as such, even though hidden errors remain embedded within that view of truth. Our unconscious engagement emerges in how we fail to realize that "our error is part of the Truth itself" (Žižek, ibid., 62). This contrasts with the conscious mind, which Lacan refers to as "logical time." In logical time, people first see, then construct insight, and finally conclude (Lacan, op.cit., 43-44). In the context of our theme, colonialism must become the lens through which colonized people see the world. Colonialism must be what they see, and it must shape their understanding of the past because this understanding necessarily informs how they imagine the future.

In brief, colonialism must become the total picture of both the past and the future—the way those pictures are painted and repainted and the different stories told about the past to construct alternative futures. Within this scope, colonialism becomes natural, regular, and inescapable; no perception, practice, or idea can be produced outside of it. Colonialism fears liberation, and so it structures an anti-liberational unconscious—one in which any attempt to disengage from it ends up reproducing another face of the same colonial mirror, where difference merely reinforces colonial sameness. We have seen this in the attempts of many colonized nations to liberate themselves, as well as in the creation of representative groups from within the colonized population appointed to organize their people under colonial logic.

Between Critical Theory and Anarchic Anthropology

Questioning Concepts of Freedom and Resistance

Throughout the human experience, humans have faced two choices: to be enslaved by natural forces or to subjugate those forces through human thought or human-made products. This is what Adorno and Horkheimer referred to when they wrote: "[h]uman beings have always had to choose between their subjugation to nature and its subjugation to the self" (Adorno and Horkheimer, *Dialectic of Enlightenment* 2002, 25). This brings the dialectic of both freedom and subjugation into the discussion; witnessing one gives meaning to the other in the experience of the self. For example, a person who has known freedom can understand subjugation through that freedom and vice versa.

Lefebvre provides us with an interesting mediating concept between the daily resistance to subjugation and the feeling of possessing a specific type of freedom, whether material (such as food) or non-material (such as time). For him, owning and enjoying leisure reflects a kind of "critique of the everyday [that] plays an integral part in the every day" (Lefebvre 1991, 61). However, having access to time or material resources, such as food, does not necessarily indicate the intellectual form of freedom required to liberate human consciousness. Instead, it is a kind of freedom granted by others, those who dominate the socioeconomic system.

From an anarchist viewpoint, radical thinking about constructing freedom and practicing liberation may require imagining freedom based on concepts such as "self-organization" and "direct democracy," as well as other ideas historically associated with classical anarchism. These concepts, as the anarchist scholar Graeber argues, extended their influence during the globalization era to shape "radical movements of all kinds everywhere" (Graeber, *Fragments of an Anarchist Anthropology* 2004, 2). What is unique about this perspective, in an age where it is widely promoted that it is impossible to imagine a human community organized without modern statehood, is that the path to freedom cannot be achieved through a despotic or policing system (ibid., 7) such as the systems of control deployed by Israel against Palestinians, or a collaborating regime with Israel that seeks to achieve liberation or secure freedoms.

Anarchic anthropology is particularly useful, as noted in James C. Scott's approach, for initiating resistance through small-scale actions, such as peasant lifestyles, simple "weapons of the weak," or even possibilities of living without formal governance, as discussed in his book *The Art of Not Being Governed* (2009). These arguments help to genealogically explore the potential for an original mode of living in Palestine, one based on self-regulation and rebellion against external authority, that is, authority external to the Palestinian collective self.

Unlike Graeber's illustration, Fromm's analysis of the historical development of the concept of freedom and the position of the free human being reveals that this aspect (i.e., freedom) is subject to the historical context and its dynamics, as well as to the key actors who shape it. These factors vary from one era to another. Fromm questions whether "submission" is inherent in human nature, even while recognizing an "innate desire for freedom" (Fromm, *Fear of Freedom* 1960, 4).

While reading Hobbes, Fromm supposes that the human logic of "self-interest" is composed of elements such as a thirst for "power and hostility" (ibid., 5). By examining the driving psychological forces within the human being, Fromm explores how various aspects of human life, shaped through historical evolution, emerge in relation to the surrounding socioeconomic context. In this regard, one can imagine the evolutionary trajectory of human will and collective agency, whether through social movements, revolutionary parties, or other forms. These forces cooperate to generate a collective human response to specific situations. For example, in a famine, people may cooperate to cultivate food or invent new means of production.

Due to its complexity across historical evolution, socioeconomic circumstances, political circumstances, and cultural or psychological powers, freedom becomes an aspect embedded within broader contexts. To better frame it within the context of this Manifesto, freedom must be discussed in relation to resistance, especially the form of resistance James Scott termed 'everyday resistance,' and how freedom can be a vital element in establishing a collective social organization.

Scott describes resistance as an emerging aspect of a peasant's life when perceiving other actors' attempts to capture their revenue, food, or labor (J. Scott, *Weapons of the Weak: Everyday Forms of Peasant Resistance* 1985, 29). Resistance is understood as an integral part of everyday life and is grounded in the notions of perception and practice-based ethics. However, these ethics aren't devoid of a willingness to adjust to socially and culturally constructed circumstances determined by the economy. This creates what can be described as ethics of resistance, and such ethics could even suggest that resistance is necessary, but only if, through these mechanisms, such change is implemented "distributive equity" (J. Scott, *The Moral Economy of the Peasant* 1976, 157-158), to spread values of fraternity and equality among people, and to provide a logical basis for moral behavior in everyday life.

Scott illustrates in detail how life is viewed on the sociological spectrum of socioeconomic context as influenced by daily activities. Some households received income above the poverty line but still struggled to obtain food and other necessities. Such families could suffer dire consequences from exorbitant rent, illness, or other crises. This captures the instability and strain of their daily existence as well as the amount of control these people had, if any, over their lives.

Analyzing the issues of freedom and everyday life resistance simultaneously helps unravel what underlies the genesis of these notions in human existence. However, it is rather the dialectical interplay between them, shaped by the various power dynamics, that establishes the distinct patterns of both freedom and resistance. Such dynamics produce a particular form of resistance that also delineates the boundaries of freedom. A case in point is the daily fears an individual faces: of being suppressed and poverty-stricken — these may compel a person to change their course of action, to work, to discover, to take risks, and to strive. All of these actions contribute to the construction of definitions of freedom and resistance, as well as to the recognition of the powers we contend with.

Rationalizing the Modern Lifestyle as a Way to Create Dominance from Cultural Practices from a Critical Perspective

Rationalization emerges as a significant concept in discussions concerning capitalism and its impact on humanity, drawing the attention of philosophers within the realm of critical theory (Adorno and Horkheimer, op.cit., 2002). The concept of rationalization embodies an operation of reasoning. In this operation, a rationalized concept is designed to serve a specific purpose according to a predetermined plan and organizational structure, without regard for its normative and ethical aspects related to the human being. Modern society operates through such rationalization. One might argue that the hegemonic organization of society is made possible through the mobilization of that society's material "energies" (ibid., 118). In this regard, Adorno and Horkheimer address the concept of rationalization as it appears in social reality (ibid., xviii), drawing from their critiques of capitalism and industrial society (ibid., 4).

Herbert Marcuse argued that the evolving form of capitalism was centered on an "administration" designed to shape modern society in a way that prevents potential threats, including "opposition [or] radical socialism" (Marcuse 2002). This rationalized mode, born of capitalism, sought to control resources, including primary cultural elements such as housing, food, and clothing. Capitalism transformed those cultural components into tendencies, utilizing them to bind people to work for financial gain and profit, thereby reinforcing its dominance. Marcuse's approach highlights how capitalism utilizes rationalization to engineer society, modifying culture to perpetuate its domination and spreading this culture in society. In addition to that, Adorno and Horkheimer argued that capitalism profoundly influenced the cultural sphere, asserting that capitalism developed in tandem with its deep integration into modern culture. They contended that capitalism had affected all facets of life, with experience, knowledge, and thought becoming extensions of capitalism itself (Adorno and Horkheimer, op.cit., 94).

Rationalization thus serves to illuminate the process of adaptation. It is accompanied by a type of modification that encourages people to adapt to the requirements of coexistence with the existing economic system, regardless of the system's social or psychological consequences. In other words, people are compelled to surrender to the system's conditions, and they are subsequently required to justify their subjection to it. They must generate their own self-justifications or logical responses that enable them to continue living within the rationalized order and sustain their ability to coexist with it.

Technique of Investigation

This Manifesto employs a critical interpretative methodology in its qualitative approach to social theory, political philosophy, and post-colonial critiques, particularly in relation to the themes addressed in this Manifesto. On this basis, it differs from a research article methodology or an empirically done study. This is crucial to avoid over-reliance on a mathematical investigation (i.e., quantifiable conducted research) of the constructions or contexts it raises and deals with.

The Manifesto is developed from a set of philosophical, sociological, and political science-based strategies of thought that aim to highlight the power relations, ideological boundaries, and forms of systemic exclusion of knowledge concerning the Palestine issue. This does not represent a methodological choice devoid of rigor. Instead, it indicates a re-articulation of what rigor means in colonial and post-colonial scenarios, particularly when the parameters of evidence, rationality, and authority are also within the framework being critiqued.

This methodology employs the four perspectives that are interconnected as follows:

i.   Critical Interpretive Investigation
ii. Genealogical Critical Examination
iii. Comparative and Dialogue-Based Framing
iv. Philosophical Synthesis and Reconstructing Normativity

Each of the frameworks provides a piece towards achieving the two-fold objectives of the Manifesto: first, offering a critique of the Palestinian plight and struggle, describing the structural, ethical, and epistemological barriers; and second, providing a distinct bottom-up approach, rooted in ethics, cooperative anarchism, and historical consciousness.

i. Critical Interpretive Investigation

As described, this Manifesto is based on Critical Interpretive Investigation, dissecting it through the lens of critical interpretive methodologies, which outline a more active form of analysis rather than one that claims neutrality and detachment, such as in positivist epistemologies. This applies to a large extent in the context of Edward Said's approach to perceiving history, which can help understand specific components of human consciousness. Perhaps this is also relevant to how Noelle McAfee presents social movements and how these movements are created in response to the emergence of social phenomena related to their activities.

This approach prioritizes interpretation as actively political and maintains that notions such as freedom and resistance are inherently so. This interpretation can be observed as a political practice by material and psychological facts. This is not subjective relativism or literary impressionism; instead, it assumes language, theory, and consciousness as sites of struggle. Learning to read the Palestinian situation involves deconstructing the hidden hierarchies and burden of history in prevailing models. To this extent, the Manifesto is consistent with hermeneutic methods but not the classical Eurocentric one of excavating an eternally true meaning. Instead, it employs hermeneutics as a decolonial practice to uncover what has been silenced, naturalized, reinforced, or perhaps even constructed as universally accepted. This interpretive practice is in constant engagement with lived life but non-metric. Instead, it reads existing political narratives (e.g., Oslo, Hamas/Fatah divisions), populist stories, and socio-political acts as texts that must be decoded, recontextualized, and deconstructed. The Manifesto never presents Palestinian political existence as unmediated facts but rather as ways of living challenged by political modes of ruling, which are confronted by cultural articulations torn with contradictions. In this context, opposition, in its reactionary form, and collaboration, in its claimed progressive form, appear most frequently together.

ii. Genealogical Critical Examination

In this work, genealogy is employed to historicize the primary ideas concerning statehood, leadership, liberation, violence, and ethics and to examine how they are perceived as 'natural' within the concept of the Palestinian and global hegemonic political imagination.

Genealogy is not linear historiography. It is the process of uncovering the underlying structures of power that have been perpetuated in dominant narratives. This includes within the Palestinian framework:

- How concepts like "strangeness" are not born out of alienation but rather reflect systemic fragmentation in their essence.
- How resistance was branded and subsequently weaponized into a factionalized instrument by diverse groups.
- How the 'Oslo' revised dependency into an institutionalized form of normalization.
- How the socio-political phenomenon of 'Othering' highly is employed against Palestinians.

In Palestinian society, genealogy serves as a powerful concept to historicize the present. By doing so, it seeks to challenge the unquestionable through the critical deconstruction of the commonsensical, such as the PA's development rhetoric, alongside the resounding penetration of neoliberal rationality; not even a revolutionary discourse is free. Equally so, Hamas's control of the discourse of resistance transforms ethical principles into justifiable factional legitimacy as well as systematic weapons.

Unlike the previous school of thought, genealogists do not operate within the structure of objective or positivist history. Unlike objectivity-aiming, recounting arched timelines with sober details and cold, performing evidence, juxtaposed snapshots of emotion-diffused scenes, obscured frame by frame, to peering eyes nimbly gliding through soft coverings of historical static. This is all aimed at achieving epistemological transparency and providing knowledge, which enables us to understand that neutrality can also be a form of complicity in the historical crime of colonization.

iii. Comparative and Dialogue–Based Framing

Creating a global context for the Palestinian condition, as outlined in this Manifesto, is achieved through comparative analysis and dialogue-based framing. The phenomena of resistance, decolonization, and liberation are not only apparent in the Palestinian context; they are also universal and relevant to numerous other contexts. The Manifesto situates Palestine not as an exceptional and isolated case but draws lessons from other anti-colonial struggles, such as South Africa's post-apartheid negotiations or Algeria's post-French reconstruction, placing Palestine within a global archive of resistance.

This reasoning does not intend to draw comparisons through classic analogy. Moreover, it does not phrase this in the manner of "Palestine is like South Africa." Instead, it engages in dialogue-based comparison to make overlooked points. For instance, South Africa's TRC is used not to advocate mimicry but to illustrate how ethics and memory can be weaponized and emancipated.

This method of comparativism is also applicable in initiating dialogue across ideological divides. The Manifesto is neither Marxist, liberal, nor Islamist; instead, it presents a dialectical reading of these traditions that exposes their insights and limitations. This dynamic also allows us to preempt criticism of the 'no single tradition for liberation' argument, which is presented in the final section of Chapter III.

iv. Philosophical Synthesis and Reconstructing Normativity

One final approach taken is philosophical synthesis, which refers to the combination of different frameworks to create new normative perspectives. This is especially relevant because the goal of the Manifesto is to move beyond critiquing structures to defining an ethical and political picture of Palestinian liberation. It is guided by Hegel's self-realization, Deleuze's concepts of difference and repetition, Levinas' ethical demand for the Other, and James C. Scott's notion of everyday resistance, but not in a dogmatic manner.

Instead of framing the issue using a single theory, the Manifesto employs what could be thought of as strategic eclecticism, utilizing different traditions to address various analytical challenges. Class, together with neoliberalism, is approached through the Marxist political economy; fear, repression, and strangeness are examined through psychoanalytic lenses; anarchist theory provides models of organizing decentralization; and a decolonial revolutionary way of thinking reconceptualizes the production of knowledge.

Most importantly, these do not simply get "applied" to Palestine. They get engaged with, interrogated, and sometimes contested. The aim is not the synthesis of competing frameworks but rather normative clarity: What is the value framework for Palestinian self-organization and self-determination? How can resistance be ethical but practical?

What does freedom mean in the context of its constant opposition to colonialism, capitalism, and socio-psychological wretchedness (remembering Fanon's *The Wretched of the Earth*)?

Constructions (i.e., resistance, liberation, power, etc.) require more genealogical, as well as critical, inquiry, which can be coupled with decolonial epistemologies, for example, but not limited to, an extracted concept by digging into the decolonial philosophies of Edward Said and Frantz Fanon. These epistemologies must lead to or contribute to designing a path of resistance, or at least rebellion, if not insubordination, starting from a knowledge-based form of rebellion and progressing into a more practical form of any of these.

The method here addresses the problems of Palestinian society by critically examining the condition of a dependent civilization and the misguided path to self-building (e.g., the Oslo Accords and their aftermath as impediments to the self-building process). Specifically, this must be read, first and foremost, in relevance to the Palestinian context. This must be challenged, based on a strong theoretical foundation, through cases and the imposed status quo, such as Zionist settler-colonialism or the hegemony of the developmental tendency resulting from neoliberalism, which has locally collaborated with a weak and reactionary nationalist narrative. This challenge must also be examined in daily life practices, social traditions of living, and techniques of autonomy for Palestinians, and furthermore. This should lead us to question not only what exists and is imposed in reality but also what should be when we criticize and think outside the bubbles of that imposed reality.

The sources originate from a range of radical intellectual traditions, including Adorno and Horkheimer's critical theory, Graeber and Scott's anarchist anthropology, Marx and Fanon's Marxism, Levinas and Kristeva's existential phenomenology, and decolonial thought from various academic discussions. This is not by accident. Each tradition offers a distinct understanding of Palestine or at least provides a starting point for studying a phenomenon related to the case of Palestine. For instance, postcolonial theory helps in understanding how global hierarchies structure local power dynamics. At the same time, anarchist anthropology offers a theory of decentralized resistance, which is crucial for envisioning alternatives to both authoritarian states and liberal NGOism.

It is more accurate to classify the work as a critical Manifesto that combines political critique, philosophical reflection, and strategic vision. It is not an ethnography or a political science debate; instead, it intentionally occupies the space between a theoretical illustration and an applied critique, intervening both in perception and materially in the struggle for Palestinian self-liberation.

This investigation will be qualitatively conducted through several steps. First, it is based on studying different analytical perspectives on concepts such as resistance, freedom, and power, drawing from mainstream schools of thought, including postcolonialism, psychoanalysis, decolonial theory, critical theory, and anarchist anthropology. These perspectives will inform the theoretical framework. Second, the body will be divided into two chapters: Chapter I (*Freedom and Resistance in the Palestinian Context: Types of Praxis*) and Chapter II (*How Palestine Cannot be Liberated without a Situating Civilization in the World's Current Context*). This chapter explores the distortion and politicization of freedom and resistance in the Palestinian context. It employs critical interpretive inquiry and philosophical synthesis, drawing on the works of Hegel, Marx, Fromm, and Deleuze, to examine the influence of psychological, political, and economic systems on the concept and practice of resistance.

This examination of repetition and the politics of fear, estrangement, and depoliticization of struggle enables the development of a core normative outline, 'ethics of resistance,' as an animating principle of multivocal, bottom-up movements. These movements have to challenge Israeli colonial domination alongside Palestinian authoritarian oppression. The approach taken here is explanatory: the experience of Palestinians is analyzed as a philosophical and political 'discussion' to reveal how systems of control are normalized and what conditions ethics as a concept arise as a catalytic force.

Chapter II is titled *How Palestine Cannot be Liberated without a Situating Civilization in the World's Current Context*. This chapter situates the Palestinian case within the frameworks of neoliberal dependency and techno-managerial political economy. At this point, the approach shifts to genealogical critique and comparative/dialogues-based framing. Drawing on Foucault, Fanon, and political economy, the chapter examines how constructs such as leadership, sovereignty, and resistance have been transformed by both external (the Oslo Accords, international aid, and Israeli economic domination) and internal (the Palestinian Authority's calculative governance) factors into complicity frameworks. It also engages in comparative dialogue with South Africa and Algeria, drawing strategic contrasts with other, often forgotten, liberation movements. Genealogy, in this sense, reveals the multifaceted discourse and power relations that shape Palestine's current condition.

In Chapter III (*Rethinking a New Possible Strategy: Anarchic Programs*), I explore possibilities guided by anarchist anthropology, ethics, and cooperative political economy. This chapter relies upon the works of David Graeber and James Scott to envision ways of defiance and governance that are self-organizing, non-statist, and ethical. The normative mode is philosophical synthesis and reconstruction, which critiques and proposes a plan that is both pragmatic and aspirational by scaffolding insights from anarchism, decolonial theory, and everyday acts of defiance. This chapter is not confined to critiquing frameworks; it outlines a local, economically independent, ethically driven, agency-based, grounded, and actionable future strategy —a new praxis. It brings together the previous critiques into a proposal that looks toward the grassroots for renewing civilization.

Here, the reference is to what is to be described as the political economy of the Palestinian Cause in the age of neoliberalism and its techno-developed system. Echoing Noelle's observation of how neoliberalism seeks to solve political problems based on market solutions (McAfee, *Fear of Breakdown: Politics and Psychoanalysis* 2019, 6), the perspective investigates how the Palestinian context began to face economization of all domains, which allowed the economic breakthrough to go through affecting the political, national, social, and almost the cultural and the psychological domains of the Palestinian way of living. In this regard, the PA's attempts to achieve liberation or build the state using the hegemon system's tools, namely business-making, free marketing, and privatization, serve as a precise example of this claim. According to the methodological investigation, this approach, influenced by decolonial political economy, reflects the failures to achieve any of the objectives of the state building claimed by the PA These neoliberal structures attempted to be imposed by the PA also impact the understanding of economic functionality, Palestinians' political fate, and the potential types of resistance.

CHAPTER I

Freedom and Resistance in the Palestinian Context: Types of Praxis

Types of Fear, Resistance, and the Understandings of Freedom

In Hegel's observation of freedom, personality reflects the human being's capacity to realize that being's self (i.e., self-realization), which allows a person to realize one's needs and to decide on behalf of oneself, apart from any dependency, might be imposed by external conditions that others may create against the self (G. Hegel 2001, 266). Conversely, an individual who lacks a personality consequently lacks self-realization, including the ability to recognize their position within the complex social, political, economic, or psychological patterns of the context in which they exist. But how does a lack of self-realization affect a person's capability to resist any challenge from the non-personal context, such as the social, economic, or whatever?

To discuss this argument extensively, self-realization must shift from a Hegelian style of theorization to Marx's style. Marx, in presenting any phenomenon, posits the interlinked factors that work together to structure it. This applies to what he says: "No form of bondage can be broken without breaking all forms of bondage." The same claim applies to the issue of emancipation, which can't be achieved if it is one-sidedly made or presented without multiple sides (Marx, *Introduction to A Contribution to the Critique of Hegel's Philosophy of Right* 1844, 9). Marx's networking of the factors and Hegel's conception of self-realization should lead to a new perspective: resistance must reflect self-realization, but the realization should present resistance as an act of independence as well as a construction consisting of networked organs, culture, politics, intellect, and beyond, structuring the whole.

If resistance is not addressed as an interlinked set of organs operating across different fronts, it is at risk of being distorted, trivialized, and reduced to a simplistic view. Specifically, when it is implemented incomprehensively within the entire context and based on self-alien-ation, this reductionism occurs. For instance, when resistance is carried out exclusively by an armed anti-colonial group, a minority group oppressed by a majority, a group of opponents who oppose the regime governing them, or other groups that may act as militias, this case of resistance would then make it special to a group rather than being a daily life practice.

Today, it is possible to see resistance, a crucial phenomenon, reduced to a scope that differs from its original necessity. In this, one may remember how Baudrillard criticizes trivializing the Holocaust as a significant historical event by making it a "televised object" to the extent that "the Jews no longer even concerned with their own death [...] spill into forgetting with a kind of good aesthetic conscience of the catastrophe" (Baudrillard 1995, 35). Baudrillard raises the idea of the "image and imagination," by which he thinks that there is a harmful impact on the human imagination coming from television in shaping people's collective image and impacting their mode of thinking through a complex mixture of "the phantasm, of the mirror, of the dream" (ibid., 36). This raises the question of resistance and freedom, specifi-cally, whether both can be influenced by the image, the phantasm, and the dramatic scene shown on television.

Television, smartphones, and computers, which are prevalent in daily life as instruments of not only leisure but also communication, work, and beyond, also influence our perception and interaction with the events that occur every day. For example, the meanings of terms such as *freedom* and *resistance* can be shaped by the content of these devices. The user who compares the content shown by these devices to their daily life activities may have different psychological conditions and circumstances, which make this approach between the content of the scene and reality different for that individual compared to others.

In colonized nations and the age of technology, a unique form of fear emerges: the fear of not understanding the system they are navigating, the fear of the unknown future, and the ongoing system that governs them. For example, how this fear fosters a sense of living in the age of consumerism and the society of the spectacle, where colonized people cannot be productive to the same degree as consumers and spectators.

Referring again to Baudrillard, in the context of the colonized, fear can be both imaginary and deeply embedded in the colonized people's memories, with heavy fear attached to that memory by the colonizers. It becomes clearer by putting this kind of fear in the position of the television, the image in the TV, which with no meaningful content, "which mesmerizes, which itself is nothing but a screen, not even that: a miniaturized terminal that is immediately located in your head - you are the screen, and the TV watches you—it transistorizes all the neurons and passes through like a magnetic tape—a tape, not an image" (ibid., 36).

Fear, transmitted in this direction, structures a type of self-surveillance and self-isolation within the factual context where the person lives. This self-isolation can be viewed in the context of the tension between neoliberalism, which aims to isolate us from the social world, and colonialism, which seeks to isolate us from our national causes. Neoliberalism intersects with colonialism by imposing sociopolitical conditions aiming at creating a rare way of living full of doubled distraction, unlike citizens from other places who don't experience direct colonialism. The first time, we live in the normal economic situation of the world's current system; the second time is when the colonizer builds its policies on that financial system, making it impossible for us to rescue ourselves from either situation. This is what distinguishes our experience from that of others: those who were not subjected to colonialism or who were the architects of the current global economic system. This is that we, unlike them, neither shaped the global economy in its present form nor avoided the imposition of colonial rule.

Simply put, our experience possesses a peculiar specificity shaped by the dynamics of the global economic order and the colonial condition that was imposed upon us. *That is to take into account that we endure a form of suffering that they did not experience.* Is resistance not influenced by this context? This questioning frames resistance not merely as a praxis shaped by the struggle against the dual forces of neoliberalism and colonialism but as something far more profound.

Fromm's fear of freedom further demonstrates how relations between feelings or statuses of "aloneness and insignificance," "suffering," "annihilation" (Fromm, op.cit., 102-133), and inferiority signify a part of the superstructures of the individual's psychology, behaviors, and ambitions based on the expected orbit of the wretchedness that demonstrates the creation of this superstructure. In different conditions, such as under the rule of a solid economy and in the case of an individual's self-realization of freedom, conditions of "individuality, independence, rationality" (Fromm, op.cit., 105) prevail, building new superstructures that differ from the ones already mentioned.

Imagining resistance within the relations of the two different categories—those who live in annihilation and suffering and those who live while aware of their freedoms and enjoy a solid economy—can bring new insights into the spheres essential for resistance, such as social, economic, cultural, or psychological spheres. For resistance, it is a must to be combined in all spheres.

Suppose the colonizer uses violence, harm, destruction, and other tactics to create a political reality. In that case, colonized people need to avoid inheriting and importing these tactics as ways of self-building. However, in the Palestinian context, political parties' understandings and reflections on freedom and resistance have contained superficiality, trivialization, and simplification, as well as despotism in both attempts at ruling: Hamas in the Gaza Strip and Fatah in the West Bank. In both places, some of the points mentioned above were introduced during their time in power, such as the trivialization of resistance through populist slogans and the portrayal of despotism as a necessary precursor to freedom. Despotism, alongside fear, functioned as also linked to manipulation to reinforce the presence of Fatah and Hamas in power.

Despotic leaders themselves suffered from a specific form of fear: fear of losing power. This fear reflects how they, in a distorted way, employed means of violence that were claimed as essential to achieve freedom or to rescue the tradition of resistance. However, contemporary practices have shown that those tools of violence cannot end fear but rather prove its existence. In short, those fears affect resistance and freedom, as psychological implications permeate practices of resistance and political thoughts on liberty.

Both types of fears—fear of losing power and ordinary people's fear—push for repetition, repeating their daily life cycles. Deleuze has written scholarly on the issue of repetition, referring to the justification to find "a law" (Deleuze 1994, 3-4) that normalizes, justifies, and gives repetition a meaning to let it continue. He explicates: "[T]he dream of finding a law which would make repetition possible passes over to the moral sphere. There is always a task to recommence, a fidelity to be revived within a daily life indistinguishable from the reaffirmation of Duty" (ibid.). Deleuze suggests that there is an attempt to find a logic for our actions that satisfies us the first time we do them, justifying their continuous repetition.

Distrust grows from despotism and the falsification of resistance and freedom that become apparent to the audience. It occurred when Hamas and Fatah failed to fulfill the promises they had made in their speeches regarding resistance and freedom. Distrust gradually permeates daily life, as seen in phrases like, "Don't trust them" or "They only consider their interests." These reflections highlight how political parties tend to prioritize their factional interests over the collective interests of Palestinians. This case should be differentiated from when political parties argue that 'we can deliver for the people that, and it is only us.' The differentiation puts Palestinian political parties in a case that should be distinguished from other instances of other non-Palestinian political parties since Israel could use this matter to divide Palestinians and signify the matter of fragmentation based on the different political voices they might present. It applies to the presence of Fatah as a political party that became tolerable to collaborate with Israelis, while most Palestinians refuse that. Thus, the more parties conflict here, the more difficult it becomes to end fragmentation.

Over time, this distrust, while we shouldn't forget that repetition is taking place, develops into a feeling of strangeness. Like what Julia Kristeva calls, a "foreigner lives within us: he is the hidden face of our identity" (Kristeva 1991, 1). Moreover, as fear and distrust are internalized, more people will join this orbit of strangers, allowing the status quo – with all its complexities, dissatisfactions, and unchanged conditions – to continue, thereby normalizing it. Both the repetition of the status quo and strangeness make it very difficult to pronounce the word "we" without ambiguity, but more dangerously when this "we," as a pronunciation of strangers, is said from a conflicting position of sense of belonging and with no collective ties (ibid.).

Repetition also occurs in the case of strangeness, leading to the establishment of societal structures that are difficult to change, more accurately, under the prevalence of the 'we' of strangers. Where strangeness, driven by repetition, dominates daily life consciousness, people's knowledge of resistance and freedom becomes problematized, requiring efforts to intellectualize and mobilize.

Strangeness as a Developing Component of Daily Life: Repeated Scenarios

Alienation can provide a valuable framework for capturing some general perspectives on strangeness. Yet, one must realize that strangeness differs, as it can be associated with the issue of a sense of belonging more than with the lack of self-control and dependency, which are fundamental indicators of alienation. Strangeness, according to Noëlle McAfee, is a component of that "otherness" that serves as a direct defining factor of the commonality between politics and psychoanalysis (McAfee, op.cit. 2019, 7). In the Cambridge Dictionary, the meaning of strangeness refers to "the quality of being not familiar" (Strangeness n.d.). In Julia Kristeva's book, strangeness is primarily associated with the concept of foreignness. Several terminologies paved the way for the connection between strangeness and foreignness, including "exile" (Kristeva 1991, 26), the "political weakness" of a country (Kristeva, op.cit., 114), and "identification-projection" (ibid., 187). In contrast, alienation, which can refer to a state of meaninglessness, senselessness, and the feeling of nothingness, may be more relevant to a different philosophical discussion than the one presented in this angle. In any case, the concern is not necessarily to differentiate between the two concepts but rather to highlight the strangeness within Palestinian life.

In Palestine, the daily life activities, such as consumption and production, the making of cultural traditions, and the unclear social system that is influenced by the economic system there, such as daily calculation and the attempt to harmonize the incomes with consumptions, all are working in contrast to the political sphere, where "relations of force" (Rehmann 2013, 5) intervene to design the daily reality. These relations of force exemplify the too-authoritarian constructed daily life based on several proofs. First, the calculating mindset that is subjected to the laws of the markets (i.e., ups and downs). Second, the distrust and the gap in social relations due to political suppression (e.g., imprisoning activists) committed by both Hamas and Fatah. Third, the implications of institutional bureaucracy and corruption began to affect social relations as they were exported into daily social interactions. This has led to a system that privileges nepotism and favoritism, encouraging many individuals to align themselves with these corrupt mechanisms to gain benefits.

Strangeness, in this context, can be understood in two domains. First, Strangeness emerges as a natural consequence of distorted resistance; it appears as a feeling of freedom amid political chaos, freedom absent from daily life due to the conditions both Hamas and Fatah are complicit in creating. Second, strangeness is experienced as a defining characteristic of those persons who waive their efforts for the "others." It's being a living factor for the other and what conditions they create (Kristeva, op.cit., 9).

Hamas and Fatah are both external entities to those who are not constituents of either movement, as well as to those generations that became aware of the situation only after 2006 when the substantial consequences of their political division became more apparent. Some members of these later generations may superficially align with either movement for factional interests, such as securing privileges and benefits. However, time has proved, based on the assessment of the overall political case, that even those who benefited from the case of the political chaos were also impacted by the general division; plenty of Palestinians, who felt isolated from the dispute between both parties and felt alienated by their actions (al-Omari, *Palestinian Politics Are More Divided Than Ever* 2021).

Considering this claim within the framework of strangeness highlights a new form of strangers, particularly those isolated community members. Furthermore, over time and through the repetition of practices, those strangers shape a consistent position as strangers in a composed political reality imposed by Hamas and Fatah, albeit with a barely noticeable political stance.

The positions of these factions and those isolated individuals have undergone modifications in their meanings and tendencies regarding freedom and resistance. Despite the daily life resistance by Palestinians against Israeli attacks, closures, and other policies, this resistance still surfaces less active. Moreover, Palestinians struggle, in the form of resistance, against the existing fragile and oppressive socioeconomic circumstances managed by the PA, beginning from their skeptical view of the PA reaching any solid opponent they may raise against it, such as the PA's trying to implement social insurance, which was met by refusal (Ashly 2018).

The effectiveness of these softer forms of resistance, evident through their repetition, lies in their ability to inform a new strategy. This strategy must reinforce the regime change, reject contemporary conditions, and contribute to building long-term strategic actions that emancipate them from this oppression. The absence of this strategy means that there is a form of adaptation that belongs to one of the forms of strangeness discussed above. This form facilitates the imposing of more oppressive procedures by either the Israeli side or the PA in Palestinian daily life. Adaptation, in Adorno's conception, serves as a "pre-condition of power" (T. W. Adorno 2001, 26) that depends on "coarseness, insensibility and violence needed to exert domination" (ibid.). Such characteristics are necessary to lay the groundwork for domination, and insensitivity seems to allow events – indicators of domination – to take place in the weak people's lifestyles. Coarseness appears to be a natural element in life, and violence should give fear its meaning. These elements are the result of the complex relations between rationalizing reality, while strangeness is a symptom of this process.

In the Palestinian context, there is a notable lack of understanding, as evidenced by the incapacity to comprehend oneself, the nation's collective interests, and various proposed solutions for improving the miserable living conditions, as expressed in the publications of Palestinian intellectuals and thinkers. This is also reflected in the political sphere, where decisions and tactics are formulated. This is an indication of how life becomes automatic and rationalized by the rationality of several dynamics, such as Israeli–PA coordination and Hamas's previous tyranny.[4]

That over-designing of reality imposes concepts of freedom and resistance to function in a reality composed of insensibility, strangeness,

---

4 Although Hamas is no longer in place of power as it was in the past, due to the war began in 2023.

and coarseness, which puts the oppressor in a position of power and the oppressed in a position of encounter. In this reality, "life itself appears only as a means of life" (Lefebvre 1991, 95). This strangeness allows for control, which is fostered by the creation of insensibility, coarseness, and so on, to influence even actions related to freedom and resistance. Consequently, the controlling force can predict and contain these actions. For example, during the war on Gaza, Israel used tactics endeavoring to influence and press resistance groups, trying to shape their political responses and determine the peak of their resistance-based reactions.

Insensibility can emerge in the absence of any progress during the war or in the post-war era. Indeed, resistance was achieved globally, bringing the Palestinian Cause back to the forefront of the world's politics; however, internal challenges of resistance persisted. This affected people's emotions and hopes since it didn't reflect a reinforcement of the making of social justice or building a revolutionary civilization, such as a lifestyle based on a "moral economy" (Scott, op.cit.1976) free of exploitation, rupture of social unity, and other destructive factors can affect society's totality. When resistance contributes to building a revolutionary civilization and achieving social justice, it can reframe the considerations of freedom and resist the PA's reactionary perception.

Strangeness arises from the two different paths Palestinians are trapped in between. It shapes their incapacity to understand the context in which they are subjected, where they are dependent, and their dependency reflects a civilizational crisis built on an inharmonious economic system. Particularly, the economic Paris Protocol made the PA the only Palestinian institution in a state economically reliant on Israel (Raghad Azzam Injass 2017). This dependency reflects a wider dilemma associated with the Palestinian economic activity and productivity dependent on the Israeli independent economic system and plans (Gaza–Jericho Agreement 1994).

While the Israeli occupation is primarily responsible for this economic dependency of Palestinians, the PA also bears responsibility for stopping what complicates this dependency or mitigating it through new strategies for building the economy. The PA could explore alternatives, such as enhancing the agricultural and industrial sectors. This could bring alternative plans for building an agrarian economy, various industrial production, and further development. Yet, the PA has primarily constructed its economy based on Israeli designs, compounded by internal corruption, undemocratic practices, and mismanagement.

Arendt suggests that economics, by observing human behaviors within groups and gatherings, has introduced a scientific perspective to understanding certain aspects of ethics and politics. That perspective became clear in the modern age. She says:

> economics—until the modern age a not too-important part of ethics and politics and based on the assumption that men act with respect to their economic activities as they act in every other respect—could achieve a scientific character only when men had become social beings and unanimously followed certain patterns of behavior, so that those who did not keep the rules could be considered to be social or abnormal *(Arendt 1958, 42)*.

There is an indirect suggestion in this that highlights the role economics has played in the modern age. From this standpoint, it is evident that the Palestinian crisis with imperialism is twice as significant as any other historical conflict or crisis. Again, that is another emphasis on the role of economics, namely neoliberal approaches, in subjecting Palestinians to Israel made by the Paris Protocol.

The implications of economic engagement extend to affect Palestinians' state of civilization, the flow of corruption, illegitimacy, and neoliberal exploitation in social, institutional, and other non-political domains. Moreover, illegitimacy in governance has given rise to a lack of accountability, irresponsibility, and fragility in the Palestinian economic and social system, affecting daily life (Farsakh n.d.). Consequently, despotism, lack of collective revolutionary agency, absent unity, and beyond influenced Palestinian life. The emphasis on this influence can be drawn from the weaknesses of Palestinians in demanding and revolutionarily trying to change their political governance system. This point questions Palestinians' responsibility to build their system apart from any external top-down imposed initiatives, for example, the U.S.'s initiatives to create a state for Palestinians with no genuine engagement from Palestinians themselves. This can be seen as another aspect of colonization.

The lack of strong agency among Palestinians and a clear path toward nation-building refers to a deficient political front unsupported by the people. This case relates to a phenomenon of political alienation, which seems to be a symptom of the strangeness that mirrors not only political and social but also psychological ramifications. These ramifications again constitute the need for ethics of resistance that are essential to fight against neoliberal elements that feed the colonial hegemony rather than strengthening the colonized people's approaches to self-building.

Remembering the previous discussion on the concept of fear and merging this fear with McAfee's idea of "fear of breakdown," which can be connected to the fear of losing power and the despotism emerging from this fear, applies to how the PA fears the loss of power and creates from this fear its monopoly of constructing the political control. This fear is "of something to come— which is really an agony over what has already transpired [...]" (McAfee, op.cit., 46). The fear, which is a combination of the previous failures and the anxiety about future instability, is also diagnostic to the PA's fear of the repetition of its failures to liberate Palestine and the possibility that will probably arise from these failures, which will lead into entering an era without the PA's presence in power in that era.

Unconsciousness plays a significant role in the analysis of this scene. It relates to how fear becomes the driving force behind the imagination, focusing on how to secure a position in the future. This fear presses to implement policies that are undemocratic and suppressive, and that defines "how a fear of breakdown makes democracy more difficult to practice" (ibid., 47), when, in reality, suppressing Palestinians and the armed resistance groups becomes the reason for implementing specific policies, indicating that not only democracy is meant to be absent, but also to implement a restrictive way of governance.

It is more about Abbas's personal presence in power and the oligarchy of his power-successors. This aligns with the numerous cases related to the nature of statehood in the Arab world, as described by Hisham Sharabi through the concept of "personal power" (Kenz 2005, 2). This refers to the autocracy that exists in Arab politics, social values, and the patriarchal system functioning in Arab societies (ibid.). Like in the structure of the Arab states, the PA, as an autocratic regime, seeks to embody itself in the political context in the Palestinian territories, prioritizing regime survival over collective Palestinian interests.

Ethics of Resistance to Face Betrayal and Compliance

The act of resistance can bring together one group or more of people under the functionality of the slogan 'Varieties of Practice, Unity of Purpose,' which describes how people resist through different forms under the same umbrella and for one general aim (Scott, *Weapons of the Weak* 1985, 37). Some cases, like the "peasantry" form of living, which is concentrated in Scott's philosophy, represent specific forms of resistance that are usually described as "quiet, disguised, anonymous" (ibid.) since they lack organization, systematization, operating individually, and may contain opportunistic tendency hidden in their praxis and may align with the "structure of domination" (ibid., 50-51).

Applying this to the Palestinian context would lead to the claim that amidst all obstacles and restrictions created by Israelis, Palestinians become gradually unable to organize and systematize their resistance, the thing that fragments them and makes their resistance exposed to opportunism and arbitrary non-based dialogue modes of thinking, which is usually oligarchical or associated with individual tendencies of despotism. The restrictions include surveillance by professionally trained intelligence agencies to surveil all daily activities and practices in Palestinian lives, frequent checkpoints, closures that restrict Palestinians' freedom of movement, economic challenges, conditional development, and other policies. Despite that, it is natural that Palestinians resist these policies, even though their interactions or resistance to these policies can be reactionary and unprofessional. These characteristics, such as unprofessionalism and despotic personal behavior that may be publicized, highlight a divergence from the traditional policy of the organization.

The ethics of resistance contain traditional elements of organization, such as democratic thinking, transparent exchange of social relations, "organic solidarity" (Johnson 1983), trust,[5] and dialogue. These elements—whether on a more advanced social level or within spontaneous daily conversations—establish society's primary means of communication. The ethics of resistance are essential for understanding why resistance is crucial in opposing neoliberalism, particularly in challenging the system that enslaves us. They stand against the structural

---

5 Like that of Paulo Freire's concept of the revolutionary class's trust in their people.

errors rooted in the contemporary Palestinian political mind, which have led to trivialization, self-isolation, and narrow-mindedness. These outcomes are the result of the long-practiced concentration on—resulting in the incapability to understand the complexity of colonialism, occupation, neoliberal design of the world, and many phenomena that would require intensive research investigation, as well as strategies to integrate this investigation into Palestinian daily life.

The absence of the elements critical to the ethics of resistance creates a challenge in establishing commonality and possessing the necessary tools for building a participatory society where everyone contributes to resistance. In contrast, in societies where roles are acquired based on calculation, they are despotically manipulated (e.g., marginalizing the poor) and rationalized afterward. Therefore, people find that they are pushed to privatize their roles and make their contributions, focusing more on their private concerns. In such societies, people, especially those struggling economically and politically, often find it challenging to find their place.

To understand the position of individuals who struggle to find their contributions to society, it is essential to examine the political economy of the desire to resist, refuse, and oppose. This examination can begin by questioning: Can a person easily sacrifice a particular lifestyle or status quo that they have invested material effort in maintaining? The answer is that it is possible, but it is not an easy task. The uneasiness lies in the link between the attempt to maintain that lifestyle and the repetitive cycle of living that recreates this style. It is indeed challenging for a person to endure such an experience and make such sacrifices. It becomes more apparent when we consider that person's risk tolerance, which is shaped by the repetitive cycle of their life. This subjectivity defines the individual's personality. It provides a coherent perspective of the process of shaping this person's ethics, norms, and values.

By observing the complex interconnections between rationalization, adaptation, and the shaping of human behaviors in the era of advanced capitalism, it becomes clearer that there are intricate relationships between psychological, political, sociological, cultural, and economic factors. This demonstration identifies the potential methods of acting, with a special focus on resistance as a distinct form of behavior. In

Palestinian life, Palestinians' patience and striving to continue their daily lives despite the significant restrictions can be seen as a form of daily life resistance. This is evident in their insistence on reproducing the means of daily life, as well as their attempts to find new paths to life.

Several Palestinian scholars and leaders often extensively describe their people using terms like steadfastness and the eternal existence on Palestinian lands. Only a few take the chance to criticize the overall cultural construction, the functioning socioeconomic formulation of Palestinian daily life, and the potentiality of practicing self-destruction against the collective Palestinian self. This self-destruction stems from the PA's corruption and despotism and an over-reliance on Islamist perceptions.

Resistance is often confronted with the status quo, which can lead to reactions such as compromises or betrayals. In the Palestinian context, betrayals were committed in two ways: through individual choice (i.e., a person who decided to be a betrayer) or through the formal act of betrayal, which existed for a while. The other form is more likely to have negative results. It represents three key aspects: 1. families or groups were responsible for selling land to Israelis, 2. the PA's security cooperation, and 3. the "Village Leagues," which emerged in the 1980s, re-proposed to rule again in Gaza in the post-war era (Salahi 2024). These Leagues have existed before to replace the PLO's influence and leadership from the Palestinian daily life. However, over time, they failed to achieve that purpose (ibid.).

The most striking thing here is that the possibility of betraying leads to compliance. Some scholars might attribute such issues to psychological problems, economic reasons, or social instabilities, enriching the critiques of the circumstances that contributed to this betrayal, such as a lack of choices. Yet, nothing can justify institutionalizing it through formal mechanisms, such as specialized security apparatuses. The specializations of these apparatuses in systematizing betrayal turn it into a form of formal betrayal.

This inquiry may lead to the question: resistance to what? Is it compliance, a possibility to betray, or what? It is viewed as a network of phenomena that leads to a complex sociopolitical reality, with significant psychological implications resulting from the interactions between these phenomena. For example, this form of betrayal was directed against the collective self. In the Palestinian case, it aligned with losing lands for the sake of creating wealth for some reactionary social classes or political groups. Unfortunately, those classes have sought power and attempted to present themselves as successful, advocating for the normalization of their reactionary accomplishments in the name of their love of life, passion for peacemaking, and tolerance towards the colonists.

Betrayal, along with compliance to neoliberal economics—which is spreading to rule Palestine—are among many unethical practices that prevail and require a response based on the ethics of resistance to cut off their progress. To do this, several considerations and steps are needed. First, it is necessary to create suitable social conditions that will enable a coherent awareness (Marx, A *Contribution to the Critique of Political Economy*, 1977, 20-21) that can withstand the crises and difficulties that Israelis intend to create. Second, there must be a focus on achieving a cultural revolution, which is currently sought and required, in alignment with Palestinians' spontaneous call for cultural change. Many say that this cultural change should be under Islamic supervision, a view promoted by political polarization and ideological mobilization by Islamist groups.

In this case, it is the responsibility of the non-Islamist ideological group to dismantle this perceived salvation, thereby reproducing people's enthusiasm for the cultural revolution and supporting the construction of resistance ethics through new, inspiring means. This enthusiasm should be the driving force behind the construction of ethics, providing those ethics with a solid foundation to develop, but not based on the same basis that led to the error in perception, which, at the same time, created the need for ethics.

In the ethics of resistance, people share an intense mutual passion to harness their social energies and fight together. Third, and as a result, those ethics will help present a solid reference point to unify Palestinians, something that has been missing for some time. This establishment requires a strong economic program, and there is also a need for preparation before implementation. The functionality of the ethics of resistance must develop from being presented as social energies into political and cultural means that function as complex nets between Palestinians.

This applies to having simple social energies for a larger anarchist project. This development naturally requires time to develop; however, without creating a way to collectively (on the Palestinian side) absorb this development and invest in it, it can be a wasted historical chance for Palestinians. To proceed with the process, it is argued that gradually adapted elements need to be considered. First, it is necessary to create suitable social conditions for a suitable consciousness. Second, the current Palestinian conditions necessitate programming a cultural revolution, as well as establishing a solid ethical foundation, which is a third element.

Appropriate Social Circumstances for an Appropriate Consciousness

A narrow-minded consciousness can lead to unacceptable outcomes, accurately, when this consciousness is focused solely on personal or subjective interests rather than collective or public interests. This consciousness has a high potential to result in harm or exploitation for the sake of benefiting oneself. Placing blame on this consciousness is often and can be expected. Still, less attention is paid to the circumstances that led to its formation. Here, consideration is given first to the social mode of circumstances, then to the political and economic modes that play crucial roles in shaping consciousness. These modes are presented in relation to the global conditions of neoliberalism and hegemony.

Structuring social circumstances, followed by the making of an appropriate consciousness, requires a rise to power, revolution against power, collectivist approaches, or positions that carry decisiveness in themselves. However, like in many other contexts, the experiences of power accessibility in Palestine, political activism, and social influence are more accessible to the wealthy rather than the marginalized but are more prevalent among the rich themselves, city dwellers, and affluent villagers rather than those from refugee camps. This reflects the complex connection between wealth, power, and institutions as addressed by Wright Mills (Mills 1956, 77). Furthermore, it is not only social status and class position that determine access to power; the nature of the contemporary world and its ruling system also play a role in this. Indeed, highly developed capitalism, with its monetization of all aspects of life and the globalization of consciousness, has become increasingly consumerist, spectacle-driven, and fantastical.

The domination of the new form of capitalism (i.e., neoliberalism) bears its fruits by shaping the world's consciousness in a way that suits the neoliberal logic itself, which economizes all life domains along-side human engagement but surely based on a particular image of the economy (Brown 2015, 9-10).

In his book *Capitalist Realism: Is There No Alternative?* Mark Fisher argues that capitalism has reduced human awareness to the thought that the possibility of changing reality is minimal, as no alternative system is imagined to exist. Capitalism creates the circumstances for this through different means. For example, Fisher demonstrated that it is easy to imagine the end of the world, but the impossibility of imagining the end of capitalism (Fisher n.d., 2). This elaborates on the emphasis made by people themselves on how capitalism appears, in their eyes, as the only remaining system (Fisher n.d., 4-5), where all its perceived enemies have died (i.e., socialism). Thus, capitalism is naturalized.

Fisher cites ?i?ek's claim of people living today in the post-ideolog-ical era, where different ideological claims have been replaced by the "(unconscious) fantasy structuring our social reality itself." Building on this, Fisher says that people today face a different force—capital-ism—that compels them to imagine its counterforce based on its logic. Using art forms like filmmaking, capitalism has surpassed traditional or classic ideologies that relied on propaganda, such as fascism, to shape people's awareness (Fisher n.d., 12-13). This marks the emergence of new tools of the era used to influence and liberate awareness beyond these designed influences.

Wendy Brown addresses the problem of awareness from a different perspective, presenting the economic logic of neoliberalism, the latest phase of highly developed capitalism, as embodied in various aspects of modern life, including personal, political, and social:

The economization of everything and every sphere, including political life, desensitizes us to the bold contradiction between an allegedly free-market economy and a state now wholly in service to and controlled by it. As the state itself is privatized, enfolded, and animated by market rationality in all its functions, and as its legitimacy increasingly rests in facilitating, rescuing, or steering the economy, it is measured like any other firm. Indeed, one of the paradoxes of the neoliberal transformation of the state is that it is remade on the model of the firm while compelled to serve and facilitate an economy it is not supposed to touch, let alone to challenge *(Brown 2015, 40)*.

In this, one can notice that even the state, which is usually portrayed as the enemy of the free market, deregulation, and privatization—essential elements of neoliberalism—has become an actual ally of the neoliberal system or a supporter of that system.

For Palestinians, they must be aware that they are vulnerable to rapid and sudden socioeconomic conditions that bring with them unbearable challenges, such as extreme poverty and unstable living conditions. This may even include, as Freire explores, many people from different classes, including the "middle-class families" who have suffered inhumane circumstances (e.g., hunger) despite the richness of their countries (Freire 2005, 12). While Palestine is not as large as many African or Latin American countries, it contains natural resources (Bonné 1938) that enable its people to live a dignified lifestyle, provided that these resources are professionally, democratically, and nationally administered.

This mode of administration is critical for creating suitable socio-economic conditions and a suitable social framework that fosters a broad-based awareness. This awareness should not be based on narrow-mindedness but rather on a crucial realization that prevails among people aware of the conditions in their realistic context. This is a necessity-based awareness, and it will help Palestinians to grasp "the social consequences of their political struggle" (Kautsky 1903, 26), in which they can reflect their professionality to establish appara-tuses, groups, institutions, and bodies from different types (i.e., social, institutional, or whatever). These organizations are needed for gradual resistance, liberation, and independence.

The importance of a suitable consciousness is in its necessity to construct a consistent set of ethics, which are introduced here as essential for the act of resistance. This consciousness is further decisively crucial for the cultural revolution theorized in this Manifesto.

In Palestine, as in the Arab world, but with more complex social fabrics, the social circumstances are hindered by political mismanagement, fragile economics, and unclear cultural directions for social relations. These issues may refer to obstacles in education, superficial perspectives on life (e.g., ideological or religious), a distorted personal view of society, and tribal ways of thinking. All these factors manufacture individuals' viewpoints of reality and influence the consciousness necessary for actions taken today and in the future.

Social consciousness, as discussed, should be understood as an interactive comprehension of the network: 1. Reflective contemplation of reality. 2. Awareness of the inputs for changing reality. 3. Knowledge of the techniques needed to implement a cultural revolution. This framework provides a basic definition of the consciousness required at this stage. Discussing the process of designing this consciousness is equivalent to discussing the cultural revolution.

Programming a Cultural Revolution

The missing dynamic in the previous section is the social circumstances that the revolution aims to change. The commitment, as outlined in this Manifesto, is to traditional methods of altering social circumstances and cultivating a form of consciousness that can be described as revolutionary, which explains why revolution is chosen as the means for this change. However, the complexity of the Palestinian context imposes conditions and several limitations on this type of revolution. Therefore, this suggestion acknowledges and addresses these limitations.

It is a cultural revolution, combining acts, objects, purposes, subjects, plans, results, and a space seen as an opportunity to be filled by the revolution's outcomes. The cultural revolution should be implemented through successive waves.

1. **Structuring the foundation** for the path of the revolution through integrating people's contributions to the formulation of the revolution's bases. This involves intensive education on modern concepts, such as human rights, which will help people understand their rights and responsibilities. This phase is crucial

and requires careful attention to network the elements that will translate the revolution's path into reality for Palestinians.

2. **Rooting these networking elements** in the social and cultural lives of the Palestinians through specialized organizations and institutions.

3. **Reformulated social consciousness:** It depends mainly on the first two levels. If accomplished, then the third level should reflect the capability of a reformulated social consciousness as the most closely related product of the cultural revolution to the purposes presented in the Manifesto.

If Marx were alive today, he would profoundly find it challenging to reduce religion into an instrument for subjugation and submission. Given the vast number of religious and conservative people (conservatives to religious values), according to the principle of transformation from quantity to quality, institutes the social fabric peculiarly unique by this hugeness, which probably will make it difficult, if not impossible, to create from within the same course a revolutionary and anti-submissive group. This is a result of that hugeness. One needs to critically examine this reality and the inner transformation of religion within it. In contexts like the Arab and Palestinian ones, religious factions seek to extract submission from their religious followers. Samir Amin, who offers a profound perspective on the connections between power, politics, the state, and other elements concerning Islam and political Islamism, states, "Political Islam advocates submission and not emancipation" (Kenz 2005, 6).

Ethics, norms, values, and traditions shape the construction of culture. On this basis, ethics are presented here in relation to the cultural revolution. A cultural revolution presupposes replacing the previous system of ethics with a new one in society, making it a chance to embody that specified form of ethics (ethics of resistance) in society. Gradually, the ethics of resistance, as a project, will serve as an alternative to ideologies that have failed to sustain resistance against oppressive conditions. To these ideologies, principles were what shape reality, not reality what shapes principles (Lenin 1973); These ideologies depend on their imaginations in looking at reality, and that relatively complicates ordinary people's understanding of reality and the link between their consciousness and reality, especially when they belong to these ideologies or mainly influenced by them. Taking this into account leads to the inquiry: what is the purpose of resistance, which in turn raises the question of the object of resistance and whether resistance is directed against political constraints, socio-psychological structures, ideological structures, or something else?

The Palestinian reality entails investing in daily life forms of resistance and people's refusal to succumb to Israeli oppression. The ethics of resistance should be central to this investment, serving as a toolbox for the post-revolution era. Hence, the ethics of resistance are not to be presented as part of a rigid doctrine composed of beliefs and instructions but rather to promote a political movement with a revolutionary tendency in the cultural domain. It should catalyze the Palestinians' progress into a new stage of civilizational independence and familiarize them with the tools of power in this era.

A Solid Reference-Point Based on the Ethics

In the Palestinian case, several corrupt channels owned by Hamas and Fatah are operating. These channels link people primarily at the institutional and political levels. Both parties, having a significant impact on the community and holding adequate political and institutional power in Gaza and the West Bank, need to clean up their internal channels to allow Palestinians, if not the entire society, at least the majority, to engage in nation-building and collectively change the circumstances.

One indicator of the Palestinians' collective alienation is their lack of a reference point that unifies them and prevents their peripheral position from engaging in a collective, meaningful change. With the decline of the PLO's influence (Frisch 2012), Palestinians have struggled to find a central reference point to unify their power and prevent fragmentation. The challenge here is that the long-followed method of subjugating Palestinians and the political mistrust made against the PA divided the Palestinians and challenged them to create that reference. That difficulty is made at the expense of both the time and the effort required to construct the reference. Specifically, it requires successive levels, and each level requires enough time for the needed construction. Here, it presents an excellent opportunity for the ethics of resistance to also play a secondary role in providing a reference point for Palestinians to unify their means of power and resistance.

The widespread adoption of the ethics of resistance in daily life can solidify people's steadfastness and diversify their forms of resistance. By categorizing and stretching the complexity of the resistance itself, it becomes strenuous for the colonial power to suppress this resistance. This complexity requires significantly more effort from the colonial power to dismantle, which is inherently more difficult than simply destroying a less developed or simplified form of resistance, such as armed resistance.

The persistent calls for elections in the Palestinian territories shed light on the collective sense of alienation. Still, these calls have persistently faced failures due to disagreements, inconsistent political positions, and other reasons. Consequently, addressing the need to change and challenging the PA's hold on power through elections has become pessimistic. Palestinians find themselves without a viable path to conducting elections. These repeated failures to change the status quo and re-elect leaders only served to perpetuate the PA's hold on power, forming the thought that removing it from power is impossible. More accurately, this case, – combined with the falsified practice of freedom and the reduction of resistance to a weaponized form, distorts the meanings of freedom, resistance, and democracy and decreases the interest in regularly changing people's elected representatives through elections, which has not been implemented since 2006.

Time is crucial for either creating a unifying reference point for Palestinians or depriving them of it. It mainly depends on what Palestinians accept or have been conditioned to deal with. The unchanged status quo perpetuates flawed understandings of reality, leading people to isolate themselves from the instruments of change. They separate from the center of politics to the periphery. The move from the center to the periphery involves the divisions. There, people start to think of their private or partial interests that are neither national nor political. The situation becomes one of heavy responsibility or is troublesome, correlated to the reference-point-making process. This tendency is beneficial to the dominant ideology of the global political economy (i.e., neoliberalism). Still, it is detrimental to Palestinians, who face ongoing violence, alienation, imprisonment, torture, and displacement without organized tools of resistance.

In this situation, a vacuum needs to be filled by the ethics of resistance. They are proposed to function against those who aim to render Palestinians without a reference point. Here, we should expand from the political reference point into the constructive reference point that determines the political, social, economic, and cultural aspects of life. Based on this, this vacuum is crucial for the ethics of resistance to address the foundational phase of resistance and in achieving liberation.

Many Palestinian intellectuals and activists support giving the PLO another chance to reorganize and represent Palestinians again (Tartir 2020). However, according to this Manifesto's critique of freedom and resistance and its proposed ethics of resistance, the challenge extends beyond the party governing the PLO (i.e., Fatah), involving Fatah's standpoint on Palestinian moral, social, cultural, and daily life domains. This includes understanding how Fatah will benefit from the ethics of resistance on the ground to develop a unifying strategy for the Palestinians. More precisely, how Palestinians live, even in their everyday activities, such as watching sports, engaging with drama (Barthes n.d., 13-16), or reading fantasy stories while connecting them to revenge (Shahin n.d., 136) against the colonialists, can influence Palestinians' capabilities to unite. Ronald Barthes referred to some of these activities as "public philosophy" (Barthes n.d., 139), which shifts from pure bourgeois culture to its branches, determining the nature of daily life activities (including irreligious activities) (Barthes n.d.).

This aspect is even overlooked by those Palestinian politicians, intellectuals, and activists who frequently call for reconciliation among Hamas, Fatah, and other parties. Though these everyday activities can allow Palestinians to live a normal lifestyle and can be classified as ways of resistance that would enable people to live despite the wretchedness hidden in their lives, the Manifesto advocates for more radical approaches to living that suit investing the already existing daily life resistance, given the doubled conditions of oppression Palestinians are subjugated to. But what type of living or surviving can one talk about under the shadows of Israeli policies in the post-7th October

period? It is that life that combines living a life under destruction, assas-
sinations, daily raiding of houses, arresting thousands, and more.

In Palestinian life, just like that of the Arab, there are movements of
pushing and pulling between two contradictory directions. The first one
is religious and ideological, and the second one is secular. The first is a
practice of polarization by Islamic groups that seek to maintain some
form of power, which can be cultural, social, or political. This one is a
form of dogma that troubles daily life as it creates a struggle between
what a dogma-follower can carry in their minds and the realistic activities of daily life, like when one wants to establish a community ruled by
a religious system but with no obvious perspective of what life should be
or what it will contain under the rule of that religious system. It is just
a presented slogan in one's head, like a dogmatic slogan existent in the
mind and linked to one's fears (such as fear of breakdown), the glory
of the past, nicely imagined way of living, etc., to the extent that makes
this dogmatic slogan linked to one's readiness to sacrifice themselves.
The other direction of the conflict refers to the non-religious or secular
practices of daily living, such as entertainment, daily transactions, and
exchanges, or working according to the modern (non-medieval) model
under the rule of contemporary institutions that belong to the state or
the non-state sector.

The gap between the two directions creates a complexity in harmo-
nizing and organizing daily life activities. Yet, this is not the entire
picture. The conflict between these two directions creates a vacuum,
and the absence of a mediator or a realistic solution between them
(though this is not the perspective here) leaves people in the vacuum,
forcing them to adapt to the status quo. This situation hinders the
establishment of a unified reference point. It deepens the pessimism
caused by the continuous failures of the ruling classes Palestinians are
struggling with. This claim is constructed by examining the interaction of small details with more decisive phenomena, which collectively
smooth out what is being addressed on different levels and through
various techniques in the Manifesto.

Moreover, this conflict underscores the significance of seemingly
insignificant aspects of Palestinian daily life, whether in practice or belief.
Ordinary Palestinians, who are neither experts nor politicians, repre-

sent the majority and need organization to begin grassroots resistance. One has to notice that Palestinians do not practice a clear type of resistance as required for liberation. The discussion on the conflict between the religious and the secular that was briefly explained essentializes the need for more active participation from Palestinians in collective self-determination. Beyond the resistance movements in Gaza and parts of the West Bank; there is a significant lack of involvement in their self-determination. Their over-reliance on external approaches, such as the U.S.'s approach of the over-emphasis on long-term peace negotiations between the two parties (Israelis and the PA as a de facto power), doesn't benefit their collective personality as oppressed. This, from a different corner, demonstrates the PA's containment of the political practice in its distorted entity.

Eventually, these three points (A, B, C) discussed can be viewed as either gradual steps or explanatory points. In both explanations, there appears to be a necessity to prevent more atomization and to lead Palestinians to enter a new level. This involves acknowledging that the integration of these three points aims to explore how the continuity of the same tools of resistance and current methods proves insufficient and that there is a need to develop and expand the scope of their resistance. A thorough understanding of these possibilities, particularly in terms of how the global context operates, is crucial in the case of the war in Gaza. This understanding explains how Israel benefits from regional and international support.

In an attempt to apply these ethics of resistance, which are introduced as abstract, this chapter analyzes the ways Palestinian local populations have practiced bottom-up, non-institutionalized, anarchistic forms of resistance during relentless colonial, socio-economic, and bureaucratic subjugation. In this context, resistance is not only reactive but also constructively, ethnically, and deeply embedded in the quotidian. Arises from people's voluntary collaboration beyond the purview of state-administered frameworks, centralized institutions, and party monopolies. Such case studies exemplify how the ideals put forth in the Manifesto, including horizontalism, anti-authoritarianism, care-based solidarity, and prefigurative politics, are not mere abstractions but rather enduring instantiations grounded in lived history.

In this case, the focus is on mutual civil disobedience in rural Palestine and alternative forms of education in the refugee camps. Together, these snapshots constitute a dynamic composite of resistance that not only challenges the colonial-settler state and authoritarian Palestinian rule but also lays the foundations for an anti-cultural and political anarchist imagination.

An Examination of Real-Life Equivalence: When Resistance Becomes a Daily Life Infrastructure

As the situation in all previous wars, Palestinians in Gaza in 2021 have demonstrated a spirit of cooperation, non-institutional, and spontaneous forms of resistance through that cooperation. This applies to participating in rescuing people trapped under the rubble, delivering mutual aid, distributing food parcels, joining initiatives to clean public places, or, more specifically, in 2024, Hani and Mahmoud Almadhoun founded the Gaza Soup Kitchen in Beit Lahia. This is an example of not only a standard form of solidarity but also an example of grassroots resistance to hunger as Israel weaponized both matters of food and wanted to punish the people of Gaza. On December 2, 2024, Israel assassinated Mahmoud Almadhoun, who "fed the famished" (CNN 2024). However, that didn't prevent the initiative from continuing to provide food (Gaza Soup Kitchen 2025), and even opened a school that was targeted by Israeli airstrikes ((JfJfP) n.d.). These phenomena of responding to challenges and wars, such as these, present a significant effort, albeit non-institutional and less organized, compared to efforts that may come from institutionally driven initiatives. This, indeed, is suitable for illustrating a possible anarchist sociocultural and political lens, which sees them as collective efforts. The political dimension of these efforts is embedded in resisting settler-colonial policies as well as any local authoritarianism that may emerge.

Areas like Beit Lahia, Beit Hanoun, and Jabalia, located in the north of Gaza, witnessed plenty of attempts to support people in these areas, particularly due to the exaggerated attempts by Israelis to empty and eliminate these areas of its people. For example, the Aid Gaza Team has made a great deal of effort to help people despite the continuous Israeli bombardment. The team continues to provide people with the following:

1. Deliver food and water.
2. Providing blankets, mats, and primary mandatory living equipment.
3. Anything vital to the continuity of people's living while they are away from their homes *(Gaza 2024)*.

The word "anything" indicates attempting to create an opportunity to survive from a very low level, if not from zero. Additionally, the usage of social media applications, like WhatsApp, Telegram, and Facebook, or other applications, in documenting, reporting, exposing, gathering to begin volunteering, and organizing initiatives explains how the people of Gaza have tried even little means of communication to facilitate a real organization, that develops from a remote communication into an actionable procedure.

This exploration reminds us of David Graeber's definition of anarchism as "an ethical discourse about revolutionary practice" (Graeber, op.cit. 2004, 6); as anarchism begins from an ethical and a sense of responsibility to the public. This is what happened when the official institution was weakened in the war. The traditional political system was targeted, which challenged the pre-2023 path to pursue a modern state project in Gaza, which, in fact, almost disappeared. In short, when the institution was weakened, the people remained strong. The absence or fragility of that institution did not create a state of stagnation based on dependence on that institution. Instead, people began to work on finding social means of communication, gathering, and work, attempting to resist the bombardment and searching for any means of survival, even the simplest ones.

This should pave the way to claim that resistance was not a systematic, violent way of resisting Israeli forces but a form of disobedience and opposition to all attempts to damage community life, whether by blockade, airstrike, or attempts to divide the local community by following the policy of Divide and Conquer. This concept is relevant to the notion of who must die and who must live, an idea coined by Achille Mbembe in his theory of "Necropolitics" (Mbembe 2019).

This determination of the right to live or exclusion is made by those who hold power and is based on what they own in terms of power dynamics. Initiatives that are non-institutional and accessible, based

on an anarchist understanding of social and political action, empha-
size that people are not dependent on institutions and the hierarchy of
policies. They can take ethical action by prioritizing life and life-saving
over ideological survival.

Another example can be drawn from the case of a small village in
Hebron called At-Tuwani and its people, who were known for resisting
the settlers' attacks in a non-violent way, which can be classified as
disobedience yet civil. The people of At-Tuwani, in the South Hebron
Hills, have spearheaded nonviolent direct action involving coordinated
international solidarity activism. Villagers walk children to school
through the military zones, plant trees in prohibited areas, and record
human rights abuses as the villagers face settler violence and roadblocks
by Israeli forces. Yet, they insist on living and continuing to challenge
the closure, the attacks, the siege, and more. Their resistance is local,
embedded, and continually civilian, a blanket refusal of the idea that
violence is the only means of resistance.

An example would be taken from the case of such Palestinian
refugees, to whom lesser accessibility exists to opportunities compared
to residents of cities and villages. A refugee camp in Palestine, just as
it can be in several parts of the world, was always a place viewed as a
source of daily life chaos, a symbol of lack and poor chances. These
conditions have created a level of pressure on those refugees. This
pressure prompts them to seek opportunities and find ways to move
forward, thereby rediscovering something new.

The intellectual, cultural path, the path of education and sharing
intellectuality with others, stands as one of the few powerful tools left
to challenge the city's rigid bureaucracies and the deep-rooted biases
they uphold. Refugees face plenty of obstacles and barriers, such as
being denied opportunities, blocked from owning land, and stripped of
legal rights that the privileged villagers wield with ease. While villages
grow into cities, claiming ownership of land and resources, refugees
are left confined, their growth stifled. However, several experiences of
refugee people demonstrate how this intellectual path serves as a resistance against the fractured imagination of camp life, the memories of
oppression, scarcity, and lost opportunities, with a fierce and defiant
identity. In a place riddled with contradictions and limited prospects,

this path breathes life into energies suppressed from birth, forging resistance where others see only despair.

For instance, youth in Dheisheh camp in Bethlehem and Balata camp in Nablus have formed new forms of education, such as literacy circles, art projects, and political workshops, which are unconnected to the PA curricula. These are used to foster critical consciousness (as Paulo Freire pointed out), historical memory, and political empowerment. They opt to operate from temporary offices, coffee shops, projects, and community centers and challenge both Israeli colonial occupation and the Palestinian Authority's pedagogic, securitized bureaucracy. Suppose one listens to how Israel assaults these groups, organizations, and initiatives. In that case, one finds that it is itself a path toward liberation and a paradigm of collective self-making oriented toward liberation. One sees that this reminds us that liberation encompasses not only political sovereignty but also epistemic and pedagogical autonomy.

Last but not least, these case studies confirm that the ethics of resistance do exist, even if they are latent, dispersed, and under-theorized. The Manifesto aims to draw them into a coherent, self-aware cultural and political project. These given examples demonstrate that daily attempts, although not always organized enough to confront Israeli tyranny, exist, are widespread, diverse, and represent spontaneous and straightforward forms of resistance, refusal, and non-compliance with injustice. The function of this Manifesto is to try to gather, understand, and mobilize these attempts within what has been called the ethics of resistance, firstly to clarify the resistant nature on which Palestinian life has grown and then to try and strive to develop these attempts into a stronger system, whether starting from the theoretical and philosophical level or ultimately through practical application. These forms of resistance, whether in Gaza or the West Bank, also undermine Hamas and Fatah's monopolies on righteous or virtuous resistance, as well as their claim to be the only acceptable manifestation of resistance.

CHAPTER II

Palestine in the Current World: How Palestine Cannot be Liberated without a Situating Civilization in the World's Current Context

A General Note on the Current World's Standards and Norms: Politics of Interference

Following the discussion on neoliberalism in the previous chapter, this chapter aims to shed more light on Palestine's position within the international community. It reflects on the existing global mechanisms for organizing international relations, human rights conditions, and interactions with colonialism, as well as cases of oppressed people. It asks the question: Do these mechanisms allow for changing the miserable conditions faced by some nations if such changes conflict with the interests of hegemon powers?

The answer to this question would require considering two assumptions. First, hegemonic powers will prevent attempts to change if they contradict their interests. Second, when this change is permitted, then it should be crystallized from a secondary orbit controlled by a secondary position from the hegemon sphere. This secondary position has a limited effect, depending on the external pressure that can be taken into account or denied by the hegemonic powers. One may imagine McAfee at this point saying: "All the activity that citizens can engage in—various forms of voting, petitioning, lobbying, protesting, and mobilizing— revolve around electing and influencing politicians" (McAfee, op.cit. 2019, 18). These activities exemplify the claimed secondary position, and they don't reformulate the entire construction. The traditionality of these tools constructs a position seen as holding patterns rather than as decisive activities.

This applies to plenty of the enormous demonstrations that have occurred globally, including in Israel, the U.S., and European countries calling for a ceasefire (Jazeera, Pro-Palestine Demonstrations Around the World as Gaza War Nears 100 Days 2024). While these demonstrations achieved some of the objectives, such as condemning the Israeli aggression, issuing arrest warrants against some Israeli leaders by the International Criminal Court (Court n.d.), and initiating a boycott against Israel (Observer 2024), they have not succeeded in changing the case of the Palestinians. In other words, the genocide in Gaza and the general frame of oppression committed against Palestinians persisted. However, the number of Palestinian victims became less in comparison to the first three months of the war, e.g., the bombing of a hospital in Gaza on October 17, which killed 500 people (Jazeera, What is Israel's Narrative on the Gaza Hospital Explosion? 2023); these global solidarity activities have not stopped the Israeli brutal policies in both Gaza and the West Bank.

This explanation highlights the importance of understanding the Palestinian case within the context of international power dynamics, particularly concerning NATO and its extensive military capabilities. NATO's policies might involve creating reactionary and puppet regimes and justifying interventions in other states' affairs, sometimes under the justification of salvation in situations like when people face civil wars and extreme authoritarian regimes. Though portrayed as an unbiased attempt to avert human suffering, humanitarian intervention is, in fact, intricately constructed by global power relations, national interests, and the military-industrial complex. Palestine is a glaring example where humanitarian vocabulary is either absent or used selectively, suggesting that interventions are primarily about managing crises rather than addressing the underlying issues. Instead, Western humanitarian undertakings in Libya, Iraq, or Kosovo, even when framed as civilian protection, tend to coincide with geopolitical objectives of resource control, influence expansion, or installation of friendly regimes.

In comparison to Israel's decades-long occupation, blockade, and recurring assaults on Gaza, there has not been NATO-mobilized comparable humanitarian intervention. Such intervention is lacking due to the deep military and economic ties NATO allies have with Israel.

Politically and strategically, it is unpalatable to intervene in such gaps when NATO is directly co-developing defense systems with Israel while being one of the world's leading arms merchants. Acting as secondary powers serves the interests of countries in the global North, enabling supportive narratives detached from inconvenient realities and revealing the self-serving character of the so-called "humanitarian" actions.

Yet, these interventions cannot be understood in isolation from a framework of normalized and naturalized political interventions that are multifaceted and exist in various political scenarios or conflicts, often unrelated to the national interests of the intervening state, such as the United States. This applies to the creation of puppet regimes in the post-war era when the U.S. began promoting internal relations to establish a regime controlled by it. These interventions highlight the vigorous striving to cause harm to the victimized state by the act of intervening. This note is essential for understanding the general logic of political interference and the quasi-procedures involved, as well as how these form the relationship between European countries and Israel or the U.S. and Israel.

The case of Palestine transcends traditional notions of injustice. It's not merely a comparison between a weak party and a strong party, where the former is exploited and oppressed, as is often the case in traditional conflicts. The Palestinian case is far more complex, making it difficult to view through any simplified lens or a thorough, clear-cut perspective. In such a case, there is a party whose right to self-expression is stolen and whose reality has been shaped by a distorted identity and a well-planned narrative, both in the worldly context and through colonial narratives. These narratives result in a distortion of the proper context on a global scale and the fetishization of the colonized, creating identities that are difficult to define when investigated based on daily life standards in the life of the colonized.

Furthermore, the weakness of this party is also evident in its position, which is shaped by the way the colonial power has structured its path and way of life through a state of chaos, randomness, and confusion, leading to feeble living and meaninglessness in daily life. On the other hand, many powerful countries with advanced technology, military power, and overall development are gathering in support of the party, which is already identified as strong. That is what features the Palestinian-Israeli conflict, which can no longer be seen as a usual confrontation between two groups; each of them endeavors to impose its right to survival as a priority, then their self-determination.

That is distorted, corrupted, unorganized, and weak when facing the most developed countries in support of the strong party. This base makes it challenging, unobjective, and untransparent to defend their right to self-determination and freedom without essentially criticizing their way of life, their means of expression, and their methods of inter-action with one another. At the same time, an external power enor-mously oppresses them, one that is external to their entity. This obser-vation facilitates the claim of a necessary set of ethics, organizing both domains of resistance and the endeavor for freedom. This again reminds us that the ethics of resistance are not focused on the act of resistance, which is generally concentrated today on military action. Living under oppression, with a continued insistence on progress or moving forward, offers a legacy of resistance in daily life. Hence, the ethics of resistance must be established across all the domains of daily life.

In a world where there are double standards in how conflicts are viewed, such as in Palestine versus Ukraine (Borrell 2024), it is critical to understand why Israel has enjoyed impunity on the international level. Several steps are essential for that. First, NATO, especially Western powers, and their bias toward Israel and a tendency to inter-vene urgently in its favor, regardless of the conflict conditions, causes of war, etc.[6] This offered Israel coverage to maintain a high level of power, often unexamined.

Second, the Israeli civilization is imagined and presented as superior to Palestinians. This issue, with the overemphasis on it, must explain how Israel puts itself ahead of the Palestinians, creating an absent exis-tence for the Palestinians through its dynamic civilization. Since 1948, Israelis have been reinterpreting things, then presenting them as if they were not originally in their places but were being given new ones. This reminds us of Michel Foucault's book *The Order of Things* (1994). This also defines why perceptions on things are made to apply to specific

---

6 Whether it is Al-Assad's regime in Damascus, Hezbollah, Hamas, Houthi troops or any other party/state.

subjectivities rather than others, such as terrorism as illustrated in the entity of Palestinian armed groups, while it is impossible to be linked to Israeli bloody brutality, despite Israeli organized and extreme use of violence that manifested during the war against Palestinian civilians, and which can't be labeled as terrorism!

In Gaza, the Israeli strategy followed aims to erase collective memory and create a new reality from the destruction, starting from ground zero to impose a new cultural appropriation. This is to prevent any potential of recognizing Israelis' terror. More broadly, Israel's exaggerated usage of power, supplemented militarily by the U.S. at its aggressive and unethical peak, was to invent a new context after turning the previous one into its remnants. The destruction of Gaza will make it an uninhabitable place to live in. In this transformation, Gaza must gain a new character that suits the purposes of Israeli domination over it and the recreation of civilization after its destruction.

At a press conference, President Erdoğan announced a unilateral rejection of any "partnership" between Israel and NATO (*Erdoğan Says Türkiye Opposes NATO Cooperation with Israel* 2024). This reveals that the intention before this conference was to establish a partnership between Israel and NATO and how this partnership would extend beyond the usual military sphere. More clearly, this partnership could create effective factors within the international relations arena and how, for example, the oppressed, who began to be more known globally in their position as oppressed, can't find suitable ways to resist to prevent the flow of the effects coming from the hegemon results from such a partnership. We, hence, are talking about a collaboration between an oppressor and great powers; both have massive destructive weapons and significant political dominance in the international arena.

Merging Power with Political Bias to Israel, the NATO

During the war, the U.S. refused to describe what occurred to Palestinians in Gaza as a genocide. We emphasized its support to Israel, despite that there were some disagreements between both, which, in later stages, negatively produced unfavored consequences, such as the demonstrations in the U.S. and accusations of complicity in killing Palestinian civilians through arming Israel. This demonstrates the significant efforts made by pro-Palestinians in their respective positions. In this regard, there are two domains to be discussed: first, Nietzsche's conception of the will to power and its decisiveness and how this will play a central role in shaping reality.

Conversely, Palestinians, who lack this will to power, represent the object of the will, those Palestinians who do not enjoy the same degree of support on the different levels, including military aid. They don't only suffer from occupation, siege, and geographical segregation; they are also forced to adapt specific ideas, lifestyles, and ways of acting. This fact has had implications for their psychologies, expectations, ambitions, and coping strategies. All these are presented together as a mode of civilization but as a dependent civilization since their relations of production, commercial dealings, and agricultural regulations are dependent on an externality outside their context. It is even functioning based on the occupation's logic, which is restrictive and oppressive. Consequently, Palestinians, according to this dependent civilization, represent simplicity and stupid spontaneity and must be the object of rationalization, adaptation, and readjustment to the colonial civilizing policies.

Second, Israelis, positioned as representatives of a European and Western lifestyle, often preferred to be in the Middle East as a representation of Europe rather than being located within European geography. To reinforce this image, Israel has intensified its efforts to make the place resemble European landscapes. This is relevant to the way Israeli settlements are constructed and differentiated from Palestinian houses. Israelis enjoy a high quality of life thanks to unlimited opportunities in employment, education, water, food production, and more. Contrary to that, Palestinians face numerous inadequacies, such as limited access to water and food production. Thus, they often face financial hardship in their lives and may even experience unemployment.

Palestinians also suffer within their ranks (i.e., the PA members), who insist on remaining in power even if they no longer enjoy political allegiance from a large part of Palestinians, if not the majority. They also suffer from the marginalization that is embedded seemingly as a natural part of their lifestyle. In the case of unemployment, during the war on Gaza, plenty of Palestinians realized that Israel was a source for their dignified way of living; once the war took place, they lost their job opportunities after being prevented from entering Israel to work, and this began to affect their sense of being dignified in their livings. Along with this, even those Palestinians who did not work in Israel felt influenced by the difficulty of the new socioeconomic conditions after losing a dynamic factor (i.e., regular labor in Israel) in their economy in addition to the restrictions on the monthly taxes collected for both PA's budget and Israel's budget (Jazeera, *Why Is Israel Sending Palestinian Taxes to Norway?* 2024).

Despite their brutal aggression against Palestinians, Israelis are to be described as civilized, and this claim was termed civilized brutality (?i?ek, The Real Dividing Line in Israel-Palestine Project Syndicate 2023). This notion supports Netanyahu's characterization of the Israeli army as the most moral army in the world. Such insistence originates from their capability to not only destroy the other but also to create propaganda that, first, views the other as an enemy, thereby justifying the destruction planned against this other. This great power has facilitated the duty of Israelis to rationalize any actions that present them as superior and ethical practitioners of power. It's no longer a mere obligation; instead, they can enjoyably present themselves as the exceptional, independent, and moral party in the conflict against what they named "the children of darkness" (euronews 2023).

Oppositely, Palestinians are pictorial as embodying darkness and are subjected to a process of rationalization, adaptation, and readjustment. Their disorganized resistance, inability to unify internally, and continuous formal failures of the PA, along with other factors, indicate their unpreparedness to govern themselves or their lack of merit in being granted autonomy. This political chaos is a product of the political division between Hamas and Fatah, with their practices marked as political, becoming devoid of politics, and their institutional structures being seen as partial and corrupt. Both movements have led to a new level of political disengagement among a large part of society.

As of October 7, 2023, the case with Hamas has shifted. During the conflict with Gaza, Hamas surpassed Fatah in gaining loyalty from the people (Reuters 2023), although this loyalty remains fragile and far from having a revolutionary impact on the social fabric of the people. One indicator of this is Hamas's failure to introduce a new cultural program that suits today's era or to integrate the power of its people into its ruling system, thereby establishing a form of democracy.

The Situation in Palestine, Taking Power Arrangements into Account

Despite the chances Hamas and Fatah had to secure power before October 2023, their confrontations and differing ideologies created a case of strangeness, as discussed earlier. Repetition of the same scenarios and failures emphasized the existence of this strangeness. This repetition refers to an ongoing civilizational crisis where Palestinians are dependent, and this again assigns the absent ethics of resistance. The neoliberal expansion in the Palestinian territories denotes this dependency as well as the need to have a set of ethics that revolutionize Palestinian lives rather than subjugate them. Additionally, this has highlighted the need to inspire Palestinians through education through a set of institutional and intellectual systems that enable them to participate in building their society and shaping their collective self-organization. Another indicator of this need is the long-absent practice of electing, among many other absent democratic practices. Last but not least, the reduced efficacy of resistance efforts demonstrates that resistance is being illustrated as an image rather than being radically grassroots and adaptive. Criticizing practices and conditions of resistance introduces effective resistance through A) grassroots and spontaneous responses to aggression, B) strategically tailored objectives, and C) an organized framework for effective resistance.

In the Palestinian case, the transformation of tools of violence used in resistance into means of ruling, while a factional tendency characterizes that type of ruling, becomes, over time, the driving force for expanding power rather than being directed towards liberation or the building of a unified Palestinian totality. Hamas, for example, aims to establish itself in the West Bank by mobilizing and polarizing more people to its ideology (Reuters 2023), while Fatah aimed to expand its power to include the Gaza Strip by collaborating with Zionists in various ways (Follorou 2023). Both of them have something deficient: Hamas lacked the ethics of resistance, and Fatah's deficiency was compounded by both its lack of those ethics and its reactionary approach to gaining power.

Power encompasses routines, institutional systems, governance paradigms, political traditions, economies, and social structures, as well as issues such as prisons and discourses on freedom that must spread from the center to the margins. In Palestine, many political freedom fighters who were imprisoned in Israel have become jailers, with the PA as a product of the transformation the PLO went through from a resistance case to a governing authority. This shift, beginning in 1993, aligned with Hamas' rise to power in 2006, leading to a reversal where the oppressed become oppressors and the resistant become opportunistic. This transformation has led many Palestinians to describe the PA as "the second occupation." Does this radical transformation not explain that there is a constructive problem within both the practice of resistance and the perception of freedom? Has this problem not become more problematic by attempting to rule absurdly before liberation and completing the resistance phase?

It's unusual and unclear to see a colonized nation establishing its institutional system of ruling before achieving liberation, except when Hamas and the PA's attempts, which don't learn from other historical experiences of different countries, were decolonized either by violent means of liberation or through peaceful transition of power from the colonial power into a local collaborated elite. Some of the implications of these attempts were: 1. providing Israel with the disclaimer towards its global responsibility of the civil, economic, national, and social rights of the Palestinian population inside the occupied Palestinian territories in 1967. 2. the PA's presence in power serves as a cover for Israeli settlement expansion, which has increased significantly in 2024. This settlement has reached its peak in 2024, having increased by around 23.7 sq km (Nashed 2024). The following map illustrates the division of lands according to the Israeli and PA modes of control agreed upon in the Oslo Accords (ibid.).

The sense of hopelessness fostered opportunism as a means of escaping the situation, and this is applied to the PA's members or those who seek to be a part of it. This opportunism often results from a lack of accountability and widespread corruption, creating a normalized environment where individuals seek power through tribal or factional affiliations.

The 'post-Oslo' generations refer to those people who experienced or experienced the Oslo Accords between the Palestinian Liberation Organization (PLO) and Israel as a particular historical political event that occurred during the collapse of the Soviet Union and the dominance of the U.S. in the international system. This generation faces secondary crises stemming from the accords, manifesting as confusion, dependency, and weakened belonging. To address these crises, specialized agencies, cultural and media apparatuses, and new leadership are required to guide these generations toward cultural and social liberation.

Beyond that, a greater challenge still lies in determining who will be entrusted with leading the formation of these entities, which will play a crucial role in the tasks of cultural and social liberation for these generations!

The greatest challenge remains to solve these problems independently. The PA's reliance on international support to secure a state and its focus on diplomatic relations has led to a problematic investment in the Palestinian cause. Resistance efforts lack the necessary ethical foundations, and an absurd shift to political ruling has hindered the transition from resistance to self-organization.

Noticing how James Scott examines historical conditions and techniques of opposition to authority, Shahin regards that "subordinate groups" resist even through simple techniques that remain invisible to the oppressors or dominators. The dominators "think all is peace and contentment; until, unexpectedly, it erupts into open rebellion" (Shahin n.d., 136). That must be taken into account: a moment of revolutionary occurrence that will shock long-term oppression. Nonetheless, all these simple techniques of resistance need to be observed and taken care of to prevent random results or uncontained (by the resistance groups) difficult events or consequences. Additionally, there is an error in the stage of transformation from resistance to self-organization, as well as the potential concepts that could be integrated into it, such as democracy or the fundamentals of governance. According to the analysis in this chapter, the error becomes more mature along two main dimensions: first, the fear of being excluded, and second, the preliminary seeds of distortion in the stage of resistance itself, which can include trivialization and condensation in a single practice without considering other practices. The latter seems to be a fallacy that spreads and threatens to undermine resistance to all possible approaches. Thus, to protect resistance, it is sought to provide ethics for it.

In this chapter, one should realize in the conclusion that the comparison between Palestine and Israel, especially after observing the support on different levels given to Israel, is unfair. This comparison is unsuitable for conducting objective research on the situation. And Palestine, as a substance that grew with restrictions, cannot be liberated without external support. In this case, the external factor plays a crucial role in the substance's self-liberation process. This is evident in the fact that Israel enjoys support from various great powers, including the U.S. and Britain, as illustrated by the case of NATO and its connection to Israel. This support must be met by supporting Palestinians. This began with the interference from the side of Houthi troops in Yemen, some Iraqi resistance groups, and Hezbollah. Some of these powers, such as the Houthi and Iraqi groups, were not as influential as they have become in the current era, and this is part of what characterizes the new Arab region.

What is to Be Done: Learning from Other Struggles

Palestinian resistance is often viewed as sui generis. Analyzing cases like South Africa's anti-apartheid struggle reveals universal lessons, painful mistakes, and shared insights.

South Africa: UDF and the Power of Civic Coalitions

Before the ANC assumed power, the United Democratic Front (UDF) mobilized thousands into civic groups, including unions, religious bodies, and neighborhood associations. These were not only supporting arms for the UDF, but they also built democratic institutions and practices under apartheid, an alternate civic infrastructure (Houston 1999).

Palestine lacks such a horizontal civic structure. The NGO-ization of civil society, in tandem with PA surveillance and militarization by Hamas, prevents such experimentation. Looking toward self-managed autonomous collaboration might be the answer (Hanafi 2005).

Cooptation and Neoliberal Betrayal Post-Liberation Lessons

South Africa equally shows post-liberation risks of neoliberal cooptation. Once in power, the ANC implemented market-liberalizing policies, which ultimately led to rampant inequality and disillusionment. This is already the case with Palestine's current leadership. It follows that IMF-guided state-building frameworks are in place, even while the country remains under occupation in the West Bank. This is clearer in the development aid related to programs led by the IMF or organizations that align with its principles of economic policy. This illustration highlights the risk that political liberation can often be used as a disguise for retaining structural oppression, which can conceal the social or economic forms of oppression or turn resistance into an instrument for reproducing the dominance of a particular class or elite.

Indeed, the dependence we see today, in many parts of the world (as is the case in the Palestinian territories), on neoliberalism and a system of political economy that is militarized in a certain way and that focuses on a particular form of governance (we must keep the alliance between Israel and NATO in mind in this regard); this dependence and its awareness firmly push for a broad and radical liberation for the sake of achieving self-determination from all the conditions that we see available. This provokes a genealogical critique, as political interventions throughout history have burdened subordinated peoples with delay strategies, promising freedom as deferred and beholden to the political interests of elite rule. Palestinians must instead establish infrastructures based on social solidarity among their members, local autonomy, and freedom, not institutionally or hierarchically, but within the spontaneous imagination of liberation. The Manifesto, drawing on James C. Scott's concept of everyday resistance and David Graeber's anarchist theory, calls on societies to develop educational, agricultural, and infrastructural systems that are disobedient to state and market logic. It resists PA's neoliberal complicity and technocratic normalization of occupation by opening up alternative spaces for the emergence of unplanned collective agency and moral self-organization.

What the ongoing war against the Palestinian people has proven is that adherence to outdated ideologies must be challenged. What happened to the Palestinian parties that adopted this path of dogma in ideologies elaborates how these parties were besieged as if they were in a theatrical performance! The critical interpretive method proves to be strong enough to combat political fanaticism in religion as well as abstract leftist ideas or even subservient and reactionary nationalism; all these elements have proven dangerous to the ethics of resistance for a purpose like performative allegiance.

Ultimately, every party or group focuses its efforts on remaining in positions of power. Here, the nation appears as a body torn apart by these rivalries. To combat this, the Manifesto advocates for ethical clarity, taking into account the need to begin among the lower classes of society to facilitate work among the people rather than a top-down approach. Morality is considered here to be nothing more than a force that calls for directing alliances and internal networking processes to create widespread resistance at the local level, which exists daily. It is not ideological but instead constitutes a force that combats attempts to establish a continuous process of dehumanization or make injustice a standard status quo.

CHAPTER III

Rethinking A New Possible Strategy: Anarchic Programs

Although the Manifesto's basic foundation consists of various theoretical studies and ideas from many thinkers, the underlying layers of the main theoretical structure draw on the theories of the following thinkers:

Hegel and Marx (Dialectics and Historical Consciousness)

The concept of self-realization is attributed to Hegel. This is not to be understood in the context of an individualistic and bourgeois approach but rather as a collective action with a social purpose. Marx takes this a step further by arguing that no emancipation is real unless every material and spiritual chain is broken. Together, they help us understand that one's resistance is not merely an event but a progression into a process.

Levinas (Ethics Come Before Politics)

Ethical action is prioritized over political ones, with political relations coming into play during face-to-face interactions. This leaves a need to undermine and demilitarize war and trauma coming from the imagination. Such an act of resistance must maintain its ethical core; otherwise, factual reproduction occurs, which is precisely what they intend to eliminate.

Graeber and Scott (Everyday Anarchism)

The focus shifts from daring acts of revolution to informal networks and acts of refusal, minor acts of disobedience. These acts of defiance are all embedded in the ordinary and not by vanguard elites.

Kristeva and McAfee (Psychoanalysis and Political Unconscious)

The concepts of strangeness by Kristeva, along with the breakdown of fear by McAfee, assist in diagnosing internal colonization, where alienation becomes a norm.

Deleuze (Repetition as Resistance)

Last but not least, it raises resistance as a repetitive issue. We cannot forget the words of Deleuze concerning repetition, which offers hope. However, it remains in a state of despondency repetition itself; according to him, repetition is possible to result in a blow-up or a break because repetition carries something habitual, and this habitual can be translated into an act of resistance, specifically when coupled with a critical consciousness, solid to understand reality's complexities.

In the previous chapters, the discussion addressed the alienation of Palestinians, exploring how they became strangers in their reality and faced defiance across geographical, political, economic, and social divisions. Furthermore, they encounter extreme bias on the international relations level from major powers such as the U.S. and Germany. Despite the current complex internal situation, Palestinians are required to intensify their efforts on the internal front to face these created crises against them, including international bias.

The development of this argument necessitated the ethics of resistance to facilitate a smooth transition from a phase of resistance into one of self-building; however, the perspective here is that they need to understand the process of self-building before making the transition. The ethics of resistance refer to the embodiment of resistance ideas and values in one's consciousness, based on three elements that perpetuate these ethics: the creation of a progressive consciousness through social circumstances, the conduct of a cultural revolution, and the establishment of a reference point.

We have seen that ethics of resistance can be thought of as a process of shaping perception and developing a new way of life in the general instance. In particular, the ethics of resistance can be understood as 1. a scheme for enforcing collective actions and 2. a way of organizing socioeconomic channels under conditions of siege and restrictive surveillance. These ethics are proposed because, in Palestine, there is no established set of ethics and values designed to regulate people's lives and facilitate their interactions. Instead, the current situation serves to subjugate them and alienate them from their means of self-building and tools of resistance. This is relevant when Palestinians lack the means to defend their homes or prevent the theft of their lands by settlers during attacks.

Anarchism, Spread Protest, and Organized Disobedience

As a result of Palestinians' disconnection of Israeli laws, which is added to the no way of allowing Palestinians to rule themselves, anarchism emerges as the most appropriate way to begin dismantling the subjugation of the Palestinians. Anarchism, as a strategy, serves two purposes. First, to collectively disengage from laws that are oppressive to Palestinians and designed to suit Israeli growth and expansion. Second, its goal is to create a vacuum to push for temporary self-management for Palestinians. In other words, this approach attempts to sever Palestinians' de facto obedience to Israeli laws as an initial step, then to reintegrate them into a framework that strengthens their local grassroots power.

One needs to recognize the political, economic, and social contradictions that have resulted from a long-standing occupation, geographical segregations, and the failure to unify the Palestinian internal political front in the post-Second Intifada (2006-present). These factors, among several obstacles, are the most related obstacles to the anarchic organization of the Palestinian community in its efforts to disengage from Israel's oppressive laws. Elevating Palestinians to a more abstract level of dynamism beyond those obstacles and the occupation itself is critical to planning an anarchic program as a societal norm. Chomsky refers to these as organic units, organic communities" (Chomsky 2005, 133). It is evident here that in Palestine, the ground is available to establish an anarchic rule based on these organic elements. Specifically, in the specific case of Palestine, there is no complex, centralized power divided into specialized state entities that control every aspect of society. Moreover, the PA's internal corruption and fragile power provide the Palestinians with the opportunity for freedom and resistance and for replacing the PA with a suitable self-regulated system that is non-factional and non-oligarchic.

Some of the techniques necessary to establish such a system have already been discussed by Chomsky, who mentions: "[...] self-management, direct worker control, integration of agriculture, industry, service, personal participation in self-management" (ibid., 133-134). These, through the lens of Goldfarb, constitute people's collective consent and dissent toward the dominant ideology in society and the "existing order" (Goldfarb 2006, 33-34)that derives its legitimacy from this consent. In our context, these practices are advantageous for fostering harmony, particularly when oppression is used to atomize society.

These techniques, while still general, demonstrate the power that can function at a grassroots level when there is no centralized power in a community, but instead, a state of oppression without formal regulation that impedes people's daily dealings grows naturally. It can also be suitable for creating public practice based on the ethics of resistance, as Goldfarb discusses:

> When a democratic opposition developed in the 1970s in Poland, crucial to its definition was that its participants published their names and addresses in their illegal publications. In the words of the most articulate leader of this movement, 'they acted as if they lived in a free society,' and a free society resulted. They presented themselves to each other as independent citizens, and in the process, they created an independent public *(Goldfarb 2006, 33)*.

Such practices, under the prevalence of ethics of resistance, teach people about their duties toward the public sphere, and their commitment to those ethics highlights their alignment with Palestine's overall purpose of self-determination. This surpasses their traditional concentration on the individual purpose of self-building or establishment as Palestinians will find that the regular laws of the contemporary neoliberal world—centered on the pursuit of unlimited wealth and privatized societal structures—don't appropriate their reality as Palestinians.

The immense pressure exerted by Israelis must be translated into a new approach to life, one that is resistant and revolutionary, ensuring that they don't lose their people or lands without serious opposition or by obedience to their oppressors.

Once each Palestinian starts to think and act this way, they will democratize and position Palestinians within their system of thought. Yet, in today's world, "competition" is seen as the best way to provoke people's capacities and skills, as Panosetti and Roudart have suggested (Goldfarb 2006) referring to how in the West Bank there have been cases of land use; dispossession, resistance, and so on, that push people to compete, produce, and use their lands properly to produce (Roudart 2022, 12). This has impacted the Palestinian way of practicing market policies and land control in response to Israeli settlement expansion.

This, in one way or another, demonstrates the potential of a protective method as a response to the existing conditions.

The rise of the "individual" (ibid., 11-27) in this situation indicates new modifications at various levels, including psychological, sociological, and economic, as well as the implications of these modifications on political practice. These modifications emerged when the Palestinian economy began to experience new conditions that appeared to be economic openness. However, this is not necessarily the case, particularly in the post-Oslo period.

The extreme growth of individualism in this context has brought negative consequences. However, given the particularity of the Palestinian context, there is a probability that it will amplify the negativity of these consequences, specifically when this growth is rising under conditions of Zionist oppression, deteriorating internal social conditions, economic and political challenges, such as political division, and more.

Even though living under such conditions intersects with substantial elements that define resistance, this approach to still life still needs investment to be developed. That development can be achieved through spreading rebellion and organizing people's disobedience as the most feasible means to continue living in harmony with the principles of resistance and to embody resistance in daily life until it, in a grassroots paradigm, develops into a more complex form of resistance.

Grassroots movements, whether resistance or rebellion movements, are more likely to succeed when they have popular and political allegiance. This principle is a well-known rule in many speeches opposing oppression and the harsh realities of a life filled with wretchedness. However, it is not always clear what the shape of the popular base of these movements or powers should be. Hence, according to the perspective here, it develops from:

1. A system of ethics, values, mutual culture, and similar elements.
2. The formulation of this system aims to validate the creation of a strategy at a secondary level.

3. The level of examining this strategy in practice, where movements must demonstrate their creativity and professionalism in
   implementing their strategy within society. This third level is
   critical as it determines the success or failure of the plan.

In this case, integrated agriculture, self-management, autonomous
economic policies, and other anarchic techniques form the material
foundation for disobedience and independence. Meanwhile, the
non-material factors (i.e., the cultural and psychological disengagement from the occupation) result from anarchic programming. By
further elaborating on anarchism, it is possible to develop new psychological perspectives, emancipatory political thought, and new understandings of ethics that can be integrated into the overall framework
of resistance, as explored in the ethics of resistance presented in
this Manifesto.

Anarchism is often characterized by having "no rulers. No domination. No one is a master, and no one is a slave" (Shahin n.d., 1). In
his exploration, Chomsky asked that if anarchism - until now - means
no government and no policemen on the roads, then the perceptions of
anarchism "may very well mean no policemen, but I don't think they
would mean no rules of the road" (Chomsky 2005, 133). In its simple
meaning, anarchism means the people, with political action, implement the correct way of their "social organization" (Novak 1958).
Bertrand Russell, however, has pointed out that some perceive anarchism as a criminal and socially harmful ideology driven by extremist
political views (Chomsky 2005, 307).

David Graeber importantly explored that different anarchist
movements, such as "Anarcho-Syndicalists" or "Cooperatives," that
are shaped by their organizational principles and practices, there can
be a general hint on the nature of their role within the names of their
movements (Graeber, Fragments of an Anarchist Anthropology 2004,
308). The practices and their functionality shape their names. On this
basis, one may consider that anarchism in Palestine would be possibly
invented through the realistic need for it (i.e., to disengage from the
Israeli oppressive regulations and the reactionary local collaborators or
elites that submit to these laws). Additionally, the mode of anarchism

should be defined based on the anarchist mainstream, which possesses the capability to address the complexity of the Palestinian situation.

Anarchism is proposed here as a fitting alignment with a new philosophy of Palestinian resistance. This proposal is not speculative but is based on research indicating that anarchism could provide a strategic framework for resistance. In Palestine, people are oppressed on the roads and through the regulations imposed by settler colonialists. They are subject to double policing—both by Israeli forces and the Palestinian Authority (PA). The challenge is whether Palestinians should passively adhere to these rules or adopt an anarchistic approach to resistance. Embracing anarchism on the streets entails coordinating resistance efforts and preparing for encounters with well-protected and aggressive settlers, often machined with advanced technology and checkpoints. Moreover, in areas less directly controlled by Israelis, anarchism could help Palestinians develop more independent and resistant strategies.

Inspired by Chomsky's notion of Anarchic Syndromes, a new national strategy for Palestinians should be developed in two phases. First, Palestinians must be demobilized from existing political factions that exploit the current chaos without providing new solutions or horizons to rescue the Palestinianism of Palestine. Replacing this mobilization should involve polarizing Palestinians with the ethics of resistance, making them aware of the seeds of resistance in all aspects of their lives. Moreover, demobilizing Palestinians from current political factions requires coordinated efforts from groups capable of fostering local cooperation and guiding the institutionalization phase. This approach diverges from traditional Marxist models of class struggle, instead focusing on building a coalition of individuals committed to resistance ethics, which can then be harmonized through anarchist practices of self-regulation.

Second, for economic independence purposes, Palestinians need to establish their channels of consistent production and economic organization, even if this requires coordination at primary levels between local agricultural and small-scale production efforts and collaboration with the existing semi-industrial sector. Regional cooperation is essential for translating resistance ethics into tangible practices, such as through the formation of local cooperatives that integrate material needs with ethical principles and organizational structures. The goal is to align this organization's economic structures with political, psychological, social, and cultural growth. In this regard, anarchism could help organize Palestinians without division or surveillance, as Emma Goldman suggested (Goldman 2017, 46).

To support these endeavors, existing organizations must contribute to facilitating connections between Palestinian groups or classes, serving as intermediaries in advancing the ethics of resistance and promoting new social and cultural compositions. That process can be seen as the third stage, which involves institutionalizing the outcomes of the first two stages. The success of this phase depends on the evolving relationships between people, rising leaders, and the new regulations.

The complexity of the political landscape in Palestine presents obstacles to the creation of new political parties. But social movements can still play a decisive role. They are not devoid of political engagement; instead, they can utilize the ethics of resistance to influence people's daily lives through these ethics. According to MacFee, who classified social movements in the category of "identifying and thematizing problems," McAfee presents them as emerging to discover new phenomena (McAfee, op.cit., 2019, 72). She says that "{n}ew social movements often serve as what Habermas calls the "sensors" that identify previously unnoticed problems" (ibid., 72). She addresses them as dynamic to solve problems, be part of strategy-building, and participate in reshaping very popularized reality (ibid,. 72-74). However, the linking of new phenomena and social movements here is functionally different, specifically concerning several phenomena that produce, among other things, deteriorating social circumstances and a problematized case of civilization.

In an anarchistic context, social movements are crucial for spreading resistance and protest, filling the gaps identified by the ethics of resistance, and formulating organized disobedience against dominant powers, ranging from simple daily practices to more networked and structured forms of disobedience. Perhaps this is one of the rare instances where social movements are compelled to assume such roles in accordance with anarchist principles. This illustration represents an attempt to bring together varying perspectives and mainstreams into a unified whole, such as the ethics of resistance, anarchism, and social movements.

Some Latin American social movements emerged in response to social injustice and resisted the dominance of power relations, aiming to raise awareness of issues such as political inclusion (Silva 2015, 27-28). These movements are "loose networks of activists and supporters with low levels of organization in which power is horizontal that favor protesting over engaging the political establishment" (Silva 2015, 29). Considering this definition might provide Palestinians with a model for developing their movements. Given the limited impact of political parties on Palestinian social life and the erosion of clear political practices, social movements could offer an alternative path. They could reinforce political engagement in daily life and pave the way for organized resistance, ultimately leading to a more coherent and effective political practice.

There should be now, 1. ethics of resistance as the tool to perceive and map the way; 2. social movements as the principal key actors and the forces of implementation; 3. change as the central issue of the narrative; and finally 4. anarchism as the guiding program. The complex networking among these elements relies on the strategies employed by the social movements themselves. For example, Gandhi's "nonviolent direct action" and his compelling speeches have a profound impact on his people (Staggenborg 2002, 9). Similarly, Lenin's strategic organization of the proletariats in the form of a political party, as explored in his book *What is to Be Done*.

The inability to systematically develop techniques of resistance and liberation, which the Palestinian movements face, can be addressed through basic techniques such as writing, publishing, teaching people to read, public debating, and so on (Staggenborg 2002, 8-9). These techniques, from the perspective of the Manifesto, are well-suited to address both the general and the particular crises in Palestinian daily life, as well as the specific situation of the political dimension. Guided by the ethics of resistance, these techniques can deepen the political participation between Palestinians and provide an adequate space for social movements to democratize Palestinian society.

At more advanced levels, these techniques, when utilized effectively by social movements, can demonstrate the potential trajectories for

Palestinians to participate in self-organizational structures and resist social injustice. For example, the case of prevalent corruption (Chêne 2012) illustrates how social exclusion — affecting marginalized groups, such as the poor or women — can be rooted in popular culture if consistently practiced by institutions (Chêne 2012).

From the viewpoint of social movement, corruption denotes a weakness in monitoring and accountability, exploring a more expanded scope, including issues like prejudice, systematic marginalization, and people's absent participation, which creates a reality unpreferred and challenging for all except a few, who benefit from the chaotic reality.

By considering the potential anarchist indicators inherent in Palestinian lives, one should recognize the need for creating bottom-up, popular participation from Palestinians across all domains of resistance. This necessitates efforts from them to pave the way for the later stages, where society becomes more politically developed. In brief, there should be a commitment to follow public methods of teaching people and writing for them, inspiring them through various means to embody the impact of these movements in their daily lives and to make reading, for instance, a daily activity as well as a gentle form of political engagement.

An Anarchist Perspective on How to Build a New Palestinian Case

Anarchism, when applied to the Palestinian context, would require working from the ground up by focusing on little but essential details, helping anarchists to enter the political context. Although these details may not initially attract attention, they are crucial in understanding specific complex constructions. Furthermore, noticing them is essential to deepen anarchist mobilization and its effect on social, political, economic, and psychological constructions.

Scott's attention paid to the little details is apparent in his research on the lives of those groups facing domination. He elaborates that there is a need for "a fundamentally different form of analysis than the analysis of elites, owing to the constraints under which they are produced" (Scott, *Domination and the Arts of Resistance* 1990, 19). This is probably one of the most valuable additions that align with anarchism in the illustrated early stage of anarchism, rejecting hierarchy and governance.

Scott attempts to provide a non-elitist argument, given that in the Palestinian context, one can see that the dilemma is not only presented in the existence of Zionist Imperialism but also within the problem: "{a} t the top are those who give orders to virtually all and take none; at the bottom are those who take orders from virtually anyone and give orders to none" (ibid., 23).

People at the bottom of the socioeconomic hierarchy should aim to dismantle the elitist control over power sources and resist conditions like ignorance made through fragile education, extreme poverty, and exploitation, which keep them victims of the system. That's why cooperativism and social anarchism are both considered grassroots movements. Those anarchist programs are in advanced stages and require an ethics of resistance before advocating for these programs. In the process, ordinary Palestinians begin to have stronger political engagement with the politicalness of their cause.

One must ground expectations within the realistic constraints that shape the possibilities of an organization, including tools of coercion or polarization, as well as the anarchist system of production. This should be related to the techniques of small-scale organization efforts in the beginning. In examining Kropotkin's life and intellectual aspects, Roger N. Baldwin addresses the concept of "free cooperation," which sets a very fundamental level of a social life composed by "{m} utual aid, sympathy, solidarity, individual liberty" (Baldwin 1927, 3). This is relevant to the case of Gaza, where the escalation of violence and famine has heightened the need for organized mutual aid. For example, to respond to the destruction of hospitals and public medical centers (*Destroying Gaza's Health Care System Is a War Crime* 2024), Gazans have established temporary places, using tents or small rooms, for public medical services. In this situation, one can observe how certain human instincts, such as fraternity and spontaneous participation for the greater good, emerge.

This examination aims to explore the potential for people's cooperation to evolve into a form of social anarchism, particularly in times of unusual circumstances (e.g., war or catastrophes). The obstacle to this transformation remains in the difficulty of making this cooperation free from political rule and open for all within regions dominated by groups like Hamas. The answer mainly depends on noticing this cooperation as an "organized movement, {in which} anarchist ideas are held by many people in all classes of society and are expressed in a great variety of activities, modifying and directing {...}" (Roger N. Baldwin 1927, 11).

When people participate and cooperate with their leaders, they actively contribute to shaping the societal mainstream, fostering widespread cooperation among society's members. Such cooperation persists beyond the laws of the market and the economic system, including the principles of supply and demand. People in Gaza profoundly suffered from famine, lack of clean water, and so on. Does keeping the capitalist laws and the laws of the market rescue anyone from famine or genocide? Not necessarily; the reservation of these laws may only delay death slightly for those who own the products and resources.

In the West Bank, the situation is highly different. Exploitation and the pursuit of enormous profits persisted among wealthy class members. At the same time, the poor became poorer, and some middleclass members fell into poverty due to their inability to cope with the situation. How would cooperation in such a case be? How would life not be monetized even during the war and the genocide?

These particular events in the history of the struggle in Palestine underscore the need to reemphasize the importance of examining the Palestinian collective self from multiple perspectives as a cornerstone of cooperative efforts, and this is highly beneficial for reorganizing Palestinian collectivism. Just as "participatory democracy" is closely linked to the creation of economics (Jenna Allard 2008, 48), cooperation can serve as a foundation for developing a new strategy for economic growth. Parallel to this, cooperation can indicate that there is a high level of democracy, as David Schweickart presented in debating with Michael Albert (Jenna Allard 2008, 50).

Cooperation thus helps reinforce dialogue to create a foundation empowered by democratic principles for Palestinian collective participation, and this is ultimately necessary for building on the same ethical foundation of resistance. However, in Schweickart's presentation, some rules and tasks are assigned to the government. Thus, the problem may develop from following the same scheme of Schweickart's theory of economic democracy, especially in the Palestinian context, which stems from the fact that there can be no Palestinian government. In contrast, Palestinian territories are still occupied by Israelis.

Alternatively, there should be organic units that cooperate to serve Palestinians. They should divide the daily responsibilities based on systematizing their obligations to the tasks carried out by individuals, each serving in their position (e.g., a farmer, cashier, worker, etc.). Moreover, another instance of the impossibility of creating a self-independent government under the prevailing Israeli occupation can be illustrated by observing the behavior of the PA as an example of the claim.

Cooperation requires A) common sense, B) adjusting the psychological structure after being influenced by neoliberal logic, and C) establishing social recognition among people within the same society. Social movements can implement these duties, as they can be identified as both civil and social.

The tactics of cooperation should align with the anticipated stages after the prevalence of the ethics of resistance, where social movements succeed in spreading values of cooperation starting from dialogue until developing into networking bodies between the people, such as a responsible body of intellectualizing people, and a responsible body of leading local investment of foreign aid and supervising domestic development. These two bodies should teach people how to be productive independently, and the last exemplary body is based on the inadequacy of the Palestinian resources that Israelis left for Palestinians today. In other words, to plan farming on a few lands based on supervision from social movements that aim for gradual progression, suitable for the time, available resources, and the sensitivity of the Palestinian cause in the post-October 2023 era.

It's anarchism in the buildings and urbanized roads and lands by the foreign colonialists. At the same time, it is an ultimate form of professional organization, which is being introduced by the landowners inside their units and where their people, who lost and are still losing their lands, exist inside areas where the colonialists and the foreign occupation enter only by force. That is how cooperation, far from governance, is supposed to lead to social anarchism, according to the perspectives in this Manifesto. This developed lifestyle of resistance is supposed to follow the spread of resistance ethics in society. Precisely, cooperation, when it accompanies with it a tactical success based on an anarchic orientation, functions to ground social collaboration that can compensate for the absence of a "centralized, disciplined political party" (Coy 1972, 137).

Social anarchism is relevant in the Palestinian context for two key reasons. First, there is a weakness inherent in the heart of the political parties that affects their leadership capabilities. Second, there is a space needs to be filled by those anarchists, specifically on the level of the sociality of the social movements that will participate in re-formulating the Palestinian entity in a new style, which is based on the ethics of resistance and the study of the Palestinian daily life in all its domains and from the spontaneous to the automatized. According to Murray Bookchin,

> Social anarchism, in my view, is made of fundamentally different stuff, heir to the Enlightenment tradition, with due regard to that tradition's limits and incompleteness. Depending on how it defines reason, social anarchism celebrates the human mind's thinking without in any way denying passion, ecstasy, imagination, play, and art. Yet rather than reify them into hazy categories, it tries to incorporate them into everyday life *(Coy 1972, 56-57)*.

Hence, social anarchism is not far from being imagined in daily life, nor are its elements far from that in daily life, such as passion, imagination, and art, which can be introduced from a non-authoritarian perspective, one that is anarchic. This would make the efforts of social anarchists more realistic by integrating them into daily life, acting in response to people's daily needs and hopes.

Social anarchism is essential in preventing "inequality" and all types of "hierarchy" (Jonathan Purkis and James Bowen 2004, 2-4), including institutional, political, social, and cultural hierarchies. This is beneficial to Palestinian society in preventing the rise of a group like Fatah and the PA as a dominant force that may create a chaotic political sphere. Therefore, social anarchism will demonstrate that what is needed is to design a collective mainstream that can serve as a mutual aid.

Since it's only an attempt to establish a new basis based on researching a potential anarchist project in the Palestinian context, the focus here is more on the basic level/levels when social anarchism is employed either for the first time or after being given a significant effort to mobilize people with its ideas and tactics. Hence, the Manifesto is committed only to imagining a Palestinian future at a basic level rather than providing a complete picture at later levels. Yet, it is sometimes necessary to follow up on the conclusions of some levels and how they can extend their effects to other constructions. For instance, the issue of cooperation in the economic domain can affect social lifestyles and people's collective political orientation, leading society to adopt either a revolutionary or a conservative perspective. Hence, it is thought that the flow of anarchist principles into practices and ideas in society can enrich Palestinians' positions with more revolutionary tendencies.

The first step towards establishing a socially oriented anarchist movement is to develop an argument on a specific phenomenon or group of phenomena that can be presented to the public. Then, following techniques of "prefigurative politics," certain practices and methods need to be implemented to produce new spheres for new actions and programs. Viviana Asara and Giorgos Kallis provide an example of what is known as "unlikely alliances," a sphere where various influential actors converge. This is relevant to how a gathering may contain: "the Association of Students' Parents, environmental groups, and the Neighbourhood Association, which the activists joined to enable them" (Kallis 2023, 15) to work.

In a Palestinian future scenario, this can facilitate the work of those actors who will emerge in the post-social movement's activism era, when more cooperative and anarchist groups altogether carry societal responsibilities and begin to collaborate in shaping the overall new construction. To reveal the substance of this construction, one may learn from *Beautiful Trouble: A Toolbox for Revolution*. Both authors offer a perspective to provide a new strategy of considering that the fundamentally created ground is supposed to establish relations in society, which can be already identified as fragile; the thing that will force to find a technique of self-preservation to avoid damage that can be caused by "confrontation with harmful narratives and beliefs" (*Beautiful Trouble*

2012, 171). In this toolbox, which weights a map for navigating the road, the authors provide tactics to act accordingly, principles to follow, theories to understand, and case studies to learn from. Each of these exists on the right side of each page, aiming to quickly advise activists, movements, and groups on what to do in cases that are similar to the written cases in the toolbox.

The push to work for finding a way of regulating new tools of communicating and gathering increased after the war on Gaza in October 2023. Palestinians gradually lose geographical control over Palestinian territories, and this affects the material potential to re-group and re-unite, causing more rupture and a distance between political ambitions, collective ambitions, and expectations for the future. Based on this increased push, or for greater accuracy, the new variables that require better efforts, it is necessary to address them with cooperative and social anarchic programs that are feasible and suitable for self-organization in the face of continuous Israeli attempts to create more boundaries. It should be an opportunity for new ideas and projects that differ in their programs and acting styles. In any case, any new anarchist project must consider the external factor playing in the Palestinian context, specifically the Arab countries, and their impact on the international imperialist power represented by the U.S. as a hegemon power. In this concern, the project aims to amplify any possible Palestinian regime from its main tools as a power, such as hierarchy, domination, economic harmony with neoliberalism, and so on.

To explore the possibility of creating a Palestinian society free from any tyrannical influence that might emanate from neighboring societies, one may consult the book *Anarchy Works* by Peter Gelderloos, in which he asks, "Could an anarchist society defend itself from an authoritarian neighbor?" Although he quickly answered 'no,' imagining the question in the Palestinian context would be falsified by the same answer. Since it is possible to prevent, after de-amplification, the legitimacy of the tools of violence that may emerge in future societies, it is also possible to live in a society without the tyrannical effects. Prevention and resistance against the tools of violence are justified by claiming that a permanent domestic war exists between the elites and the lower classes (Gelderloos 2010, 342). It's necessary to prevent this war from continuing, where the former is always the aggressor. However, in Gaza, Jerusalem, and the West Bank, the local authorities, led by Hamas and Fatah, have strong ties with the Arab regimes to the extent that this affected their policies. Some Palestinians would even think of the PA as a simulation of the Arab despotic regime (al-Omari, *How the Palestinian Authority Failed Its People* 2023).

Two considerations arise in responding to this issue. First, it is essential to combat the seeds of building a tyrannical power that may occur from within the same context, serving other neighboring regimes and being empowered by them. Second, as learned from Gelderloos, it is essential to create a group of militias that prevent interference, thereby avoiding the claim that interference is justified on the grounds of regional dangers. Gelderloos offers the example of the Makhnovists, who existed in southern Ukraine for some time after World War I. They fought against the so-called "White Army," which was larger and more supported by the West but was defeated by the tactics employed by the Makhnovists (Gelderloos 2010, 244).

Today's world differs in its considerations, perspectives, and in their uses of power and violence. Israel, through the war on Gaza, proved a new base of power-usage. It showed how people who worked intensively to support Palestinians and stop the genocide were unable to use their means and methods of protesting to end the war. This has highlighted the need to strengthen the means of pressure exerted against their governments. Those people didn't have much, but their means were weak. This point again necessitates considering the anarchic imagination of the Palestinian Cause based on gradual and networked considerations from building a cooperative logic between the lower part of society until building militias that must exist side by side with international movements and groups that can put heavy support for these militias that may face suppression from other states or regional powers.

Among the anticipated criticisms, the liberal nationalist position remains perhaps the most reasonable, as it attempts to reconcile statecraft with diplomacy, arguing that diplomacy, international law, and even the Oslo constructs offer an "accurate" path to Palestinian freedom. But this reasoning, as realistic as it is, clings to a promise which has continually been shown to be unattainable. The Oslo Accords did not transfer sovereignty but instead sealed a regime of managed occupation and required subcontracted repression. Not realism, but denial, to continue to believe in a colonial power's "goodwill" or the asymmetry of international diplomatic discourse. Such is the madness of misplaced optimism; the Manifesto's strongest point is exactly its rejection of this illusory pragmatism. It instead focuses on self-organization, mutual aid, ethical disobedience, and one's abilities.

On the contrary, all who have been calling for armed struggle, especially the Hamas groups, may find it pessimistic to the extent of considering it as a strictly pacifist tactic for opposing violence, which they embrace only to respond to force. Indeed, no rejection of violence is found in this analysis that this Manifesto espouses. The fault exists instead in the absence of a limitation on dictatorship. It is in desperation that the struggles of so many are turned into a commodity with no ethical basis. To employ armed action without a moral foundation is to risk falling into the cynical pageantry of resistance, the very thing one would seek to deconstruct. Ethics are not the whimsical accessories of a middle-class romance or simply a middle-class perspective; these set boundaries within which a strategy operates. There is no speck of legitimacy yet; however, the acquisition of power all too systematically succumbs to oppression, marvelously masquerading itself as sovereign. Things go topsy-turvy.

The Manifesto does not wholly abhor the vision of liberal nationalists or exponents of Islamist resistance. Instead, it attempts to go deeper and radicalize such inclinations in a way that they transcend simplistic expositions of political struggle. It recognizes that freedom must bring together material conditions with moral imagination; it acknowledges that the talents and experiences of the people are grounded in reality rather than being surrendered to elites, oppressive states, or other dominant forces. This kind of politics demands uncomplicated thinking and imagination simultaneously and, above all, the humility to acknowledge and learn from what has failed in the past.

Examining the concept of resistance, it is often described as a negative phenomenon. This is one of the primary problems the book identifies, more clearly, the reduction of Palestinian resistance to a reactive stance, particularly as monopolized and hollowed out by the Palestinian Authority (PA). The PA has cloaked its bureaucratic governance and security coordination with Israel in the claim of resistance, emptying the term of its ethical and revolutionary substance. Even Hamas, while possessing a different strategy (primarily armed struggle), ultimately reproduces factional, statist, and exclusionary models of claimed 'resistance' or 'liberation battle.' The danger here is profound in the overall praxis of resistance. These dominant formations have instrumentalized resistance in the service of domination, compromise, and the reproduction of the elite. On this basis, is this not risky in terms of our conception of resistance, which is to oppose dominance and reproduce the oppressive conditions?

These ethics are grounded in daily life, in forms of dignity that persist and insist despite colonial domination and internal repression. Real-life equivalent examples: the Palestinian student who crosses the checkpoint to go to school or university, the Palestinian mother who crosses the barrier each morning to reach work, the refusal to forget that their job is the only way to survive (which constitutes the spontaneous meaning of unarmed and straightforward resistance), the choice to live meaningfully in the face of despair due to the very lack of options.

What is considered affirmative, anarchic, and ethical politics is already present in fragments throughout Palestinian society. It exists not only in NGOs or political parties' monopoly of modes of resistance, as often illustrated, but in the spontaneous and often-unrecognized social inventions of ordinary people: mutual aid networks in Gaza during the siege, informal community schooling, grassroots organizing during the political uprising of 2021, or even refusal to cooperate with the PA's surveillance apparatus and their approach of security collaboration with Israel. Yet these practices remain scattered, untheorized, and vulnerable to absorption or erasure.

Last but not least, a part of the task in this Manifesto, then, appears to be epistemological: to unveil, recognize, and amplify these lifeways and forms of knowledge. Additionally, the illustration of ethics of resistance is for ethical reconstruction, for collective life that rejects domination in all forms, and for the recovery of the political imagination that has been buried under checkpoints, falsified conceptions of resistance, reactionary paradigms claimed to be the exclusive ways of resistance and their factional violence, including imprisoning political opponents, assassinating some of them, preventing them from having their jobs, intending to dismantle revolutionary political movements, and other policies. The purpose is not to create a romanticized resilience but to start a political proposal: to organize these ways of resistance and disobedience, which are often invisible, into a new paradigm of collective ethics and political orientation, beyond the state, beyond nationalist fantasies, which the PA's experience proved to be reactionary, and beyond technocratic governance. This is what should be introduced as liberation from below.

CONCLUSION

Toward a Horizon of Liberation

This Manifesto has traversed the terrain of Palestinian suffering, not only to symbolize its layers but to demolish its scaffolding and bare its underbelly. As its pages show, this work, like so many before it, has tried to do what remains unusual in the case of Palestinian discourse - disconnect the cause of liberation from the moribund syntax of diplomacy, bureaucratic governance, and statism, and relocate it to the epicenter of people's struggle, ethic, and collective imagination. Each of the ascendant doctrines is likely to be scrutinized: whether liberal legalism, authoritarian nationalism, or technocratic developmentalism, they have been drawn for so long to a cul-de-sac, providing unconvincing avenues toward freedom. Instead, they are trapped in a grid of control, dependency, and spectacle. The Oslo Accords, once hailed as the nascent promise of statehood, are today the skeletal remains of a launched project of liberation. Such accords are a pre-condition blueprint designed to transform the fluctuating energy of revolutionary zeal in "seizing" a state into stagnating managerial torpor and stalemate. The Palestinian Authority is not an institution of national passion but a subcontractor charged with the responsibility of providing security, stability, and economic fragmentation.

The cases to be diagnosed within this Manifesto include not just material dispossession but also epistemic strangulation. The struggle has been aesthetically framed, stylized, and often commodified. A bizarre alienation from the means, ethics, and telos of freedom now informs Palestinian political consciousness. Grievance is increasingly abstracted from everyday life, and resistance is presented as an abstraction to be attained rather than something that can be asserted in existing conditions. Having this in mind, this Manifesto has sketched a vision based on what we have termed the ethics of resistance. Not as some blueprint or idealized map to some future world, but as lived. These ethics are the product of epistemic violence, comprising the detritus of homes, the bone life of ideology and government, and reorganizing the political terrain: from farm labor, checkpoint crossing, kinship support, stubbornness, and defiant refusal to surrender. Resistance ethics oppose authoritarian coercion and liberal tolerance. They don't demand a Palestinian state, as in the nation states that compromised their nation, but a free people centered on interdependence, justice, and historical awareness, the foundation of the social contract.

Suppose the post-Oslo era is where Palestinian disillusionment had become the norm. In that case, this Manifesto defiantly tries to reverse that. We've contended, from the point of view of self-organization—whether through anarchist anthropology, critical theory, or decolonial thought—rather than institutional reliance—as the pivot of resistance. The idea is not chaos for chaos' sake but for healing, which requires deep foundations, re-taking life on Palestinian terms, re-imagined ethically on bottom-up terms, and radical pedagogy. In such an attempt, there is a total dismissal of defeatism and mimicry. Willingly surrendering to internalized colonial reasoning, along with the rationalized scattering of hope, makes defeatism complicit in contemplation. Reusing the machinery of the colonial state under the cloak of nationalist Mimicry is a betrayal. What is being proposed as an alternative in this instance is not just resistance but creation. Not negation, but proposition. Palestinian resistance ought not just to speak truth to power but instead build power differently.

Most importantly, this Manifesto has not fetishized pain or sensationalized martyrdom. Instead, it has dealt with pain as testimony, not identity. It has demanded the Palestinian struggle is not a stage of ongoing grievance but a struggle for the recovery of the future. And that future will not be from foreign beneficence, from dominant rule classes, or collapsed peace talks. It will be constructed by the long disenfranchised of the political arithmetic: the dispossessed, the alienated, the uncredentialed, the everyday.

We end by stating what is most routinely avoided: no gradual reform will bring freedom. It takes breakage. But not breakage for the sake of breakage. This breakage is a consequence of the failure of the legitimacy of the paradigms and the moral clarity that follows. The question that we ask is not whether Palestine will ever be free, but what type of freedom is it worth constructing? Freedom that reflects global systems of erasure, hierarchy, and oppression? Or a freedom that brings something radically humane, fiercely rooted, and collectively imagined? This Manifesto has chosen the latter. Not off script, but by questioning, by answering back as a problem to be enjoyed more than an answer to be spewed back. The Manifesto calls for involvement rather than just consumption. To be of value, freedom must be written by individuals who are living alternatively.

Bibliography

(JfJfP), Jews for Justice for Palestinians. n.d. *Within a Month, the Israeli Army Has Destroyed What Remained of Gaza's Education System.* Accessed April 13, 2025. http://bit.ly/45tZWB1.

Adorno, Max Horkheimer and Theodor W. 2002. *Dialectic of Enlightenment.* Stanford: Stanford University Press.

Adorno, Theodor W. 2001. *Minima Moralia: Reflections from Damaged Life.* Madrid: TAURUS.

al-Omari, Ghaith. 2023. How the Palestinian Authority Failed Its People. *The Washington Institute for Near East Policy.* October 19. http://bit.ly/4l8MO8O.

—. 2021. *Palestinian Politics Are More Divided Than Ever.* May 27. http://bit.ly/3G0q5gu

Arendt, Hannah. 1958. *The Human Condition* Chicago: The University of Chicago Press.

Ashly, Jaclynn. 2018. 'We want it cancelled': Palestinians protest social security law. *Al Jazeera.* November 11. http://bit.ly/4l5EUx4.

Barthes, Ronald. n.d. *Mythologies.* New York: Noonday Press.

Baudrillard, Jean. 1995. *Simulacra and Simulation.* Michigan: University of Michigan Press.

—. 2012. *Beautiful Trouble: A Toolbox for Revolution.* New York: OR Books.

Bhabha, Homi K. 1994. *The Location of Culture.* London: Routledge.

Bonné, A. 1938. Natural Resources of Palestine. *The Royal Geographical Society* 259-266.

Borrell, Josep. 2024. *Shangri-La Dialogue: Speech by High Representative Josep Borrell on Security in the Asia-Pacific Region.* European External Action Service.

Bourdieu, Pierre. 2013. *Outline of a Theory of Practice.* Cambridge: Cambridge University Press.

Brown, Wendy. 2015. *Undoing the Demos: Neoliberalism's Stealth Revolution.* Brooklyn: Zone Books.

Butler, Judith. 1997. *The Psychic Life of Power.* Stanford: Stanford University Press.

Chêne, Marie. 2012. *Overview of corruption and anti-corruption in Palestine.* U4 Anti-Corruption Resource Centre.

Chomsky, Noam. 2005. *On Anarchism.* Edinburgh: AK Press.

CNN. 2024. *Famed Gaza Soup Chef Killed in Israeli Airstrike.* December 4. http://bit.ly/44az86E.

Court, International Criminal. n.d. *Statement by ICC Prosecutor Karim A.A. Khan KC on Applications for Arrest Warrants in Situation in the State of Palestine.* Accessed June 2, 2025. http://bit.ly/3I2X0Bu

Coy, Peter E. B. 1972. Social Anarchism: An Atavistic Ideology of the Peasant. *Journal of Interamerican Studies and World Affairs* 133-149.

Deleuze, Gilles. 1994. *Difference & Repetition.* New York: Columbia University Press.

2024. Destroying Gaza's Health Care System Is a War Crime. *Foreign Policy.* February 9. http://bit.ly/45oCh51.

2024. Erdoğan Says Türkiye Opposes NATO Cooperation with Israel. Hürriyet Daily News.

euronews. 2023. Netanyahu: 'We are sons of light, they are sons of darkness'. YouTube, October 23.

Fanon, Frantz. 1986. *Black Skin, White Masks*. London: Pluto Press.

—. 1963. *The Wretched of the Earth*. New York: Grove Press.

Farsakh, Leila. n.d. Democracy Promotion in Palestine: Aid and the "DeDemocratization" of the West Bank and Gaza. *Center for Development Studies*.

Fisher, Mark. n.d. *Capitalist Realism: Is There No Alternative?* Zero Books.

Follorou, Jacques. 2023. *The Palestinian Authority's Conflicted Security Relationship with Israel in the West Bank, Le Monde*. December 13. http://bit.ly/44lnW8k.

Foucault, Michel. 1994. *The Order of Things*.

Freire, Paulo. 2005. *Pedagogy of the Oppressed*. New York: continuum.

Frisch, H. 2012. "The Demise of the PLO: Neither Diaspora nor Statehood." *Political Science Quarterly* 241-261.

Fromm, Erich. 1960. *The Fear of Freedom*. London: Routledge & Kegan Paul LTD.

2025. Gaza Soup Kitchen. Accessed June 2, 2025. http://bit.ly/463tHsD.

Gaza, Aid. 2024. *Action for Gaza: Food to Displaced People Jabalia*, Beit Hanoun, Lahia. October. Accessed December 29, 2024. http://bit.ly/3SWJp12.

Gaza–Jericho Agreement. 1994. (April 29).

Gelderloos, Peter. 2010. *Anarchy Works: Examples of Anarchist Ideas in Practice*. Ardent Press.

Gish, Arthur G. 2019. *Hope & Nonviolent Action in a Palestinian Village*. Wipf and Stock.

Goldfarb, Jeffrey C. 2006. *The Politics of Small Things: The Power of the Powerless in Dark Times*. Chicago: University of Chicago Press.

Goldman, Emma. 2017. *Anarchism and Other Essays*. Enhanced Media.

Graeber, David. 2004. *Fragments of an Anarchist Anthropology*. Chicago: Prickly Paradigm Press.

2017. *Hamas and Fatah: How are the two groups different?* October 12. http://bit.ly/4jXbdNR

Hanafi, Sari and Linda Tabar. 2005. *The Emergence of a Palestinian Globalized Elite: Donors, International Organizations and Local NGOs*. Ramallah: Muwatin.

Hegel, G.W.F. 2001. *Philosophy of Right*. Kitchener: Batoche Books.

Hegel, Georg Wilhelm Friedrich. 2018. *The Phenomenology of Spirit*. Cambridge: Cambridge University Press.

Houston, Gregory. 1999. *The National Liberation Struggle in South Africa: A Case Study of the United Democratic Front*. Aldershot: Ashgate and HSRC Press.

Jazeera, Al. 2024. *Pro-Palestine Demonstrations Around the World as Gaza War Nears 100 Days*. January 13. http://bit.ly/44bprVD.

—. 2023. *What is Israel's Narrative on the Gaza Hospital Explosion?* October 18. Accessed November 15, 2024. http://bit.ly/447A9fO.

—. 2024. *Why Is Israel Sending Palestinian Taxes to Norway?* January 23. http://bit.ly/446opd8.

Jenna Allard, Carl Davidson, and Julie Matthaei. 2008. *Solidarity Economy: Building Alternatives for People and Planet.* Chicago: ChangeMaker Publications .

Johnathan Purkis and James Bowen. 2004. *Changing Anarchism: Anarchist Theory and Practice in a Global Age.* Manchester: Manchester University Press.

Johnson, Whitney Pope and Barclay D. 1983. Inside Organic Solidarity. *American Sociological Review* 681-692.

Kallis, Viviana Asara and Giorgos. 2023. "The prefigurative politics of social movements and their processual production of space: The case of the Indignados movement." *Environment and Planning C: Politics and Space* (Environment and Planning C: Politics and Space) 56-76.

Kautsky, Karl. 1903. *The Social Revolution.* Charles Kerr & Co.

Kenz, Samir Amin and Ali EL. 2005. *Europe and the Arab world.* London: Zed Books.

Kristeva, Julia. 1991. *Strangers to Ourselves.* New York: Columbia University Press.

Lacan, Jacques. 1998. *The Four Fundamental Concepts of Psychoanalysis.* New York: W.W. Norton & Company.

Lefebvre, Henri. 1991. *Critique of Everyday Life.* London: VERSO.

Lenin, V. I. 1973. *What Is to Be Done?* Beijing: Foreign Languages Press.

Levinas, Emmanuel. 1979. *Totality and Infinity.* The Hague: Martinus Nijhoff Publishers.

Lustick, Ian S. 1997. "The Oslo Agreement as an Obstacle to Peace." *Journal of Palestine Studies* 61-66.

Marcuse, Herbert. 2002. *One-Dimensional Man.* Routledge.

Marx, Karl. 1977. *A Contribution to the Critique of Political Economy.* Moscow: Progress Publishers.

Marx, Karl. 1844. Introduction to A Contribution to the Critique of Hegel's Philosophy of Right. *Deutsch-Französische Jahrbucher.*

Mbembe, Achille. 2019. *Necropolitics.* Durham: Duke University Press.

McAfee, Noëlle. 2019. *Fear of Breakdown: Politics and Psychoanalysis.* New York: Columbia University Press.

Mills, C. Wright. 1956. *The Power Elite.* Oxford: Oxford University Press.

Nashed, Mat. 2024. *How Israeli Settlements Are Taking Over the West Bank as Gaza War Rages Al Jazeera.* July 19. http://bit.ly/44lofQC.

Novak, D. 1958. *The Place of Anarchism in the History of Political Thought.* Cambridge University Press 308.

Observer, EU. 2024. *Israel's Latest Offensive in Gaza Raises Concerns for Public Health.* February 12. http://bit.ly/4l8TLGW.

Raghad Azzam Injass, Tamat Sarmidi, Malek Marwan Injas. 2017. The Paris Protocol and the Palestinian Economy: New Evidence. *South East Asia Journal of Contemporary Business, Economics and Law.*

Rehmann, Jan. 2013. *Theories of Ideologies.* Leiden: Brill.

Reuters. 2023. *Poll Shows Palestinians Back Oct. 7 Attack on Israel, Support for Hamas Rises.* December 14. http://bit.ly/447C4kw.

Roger N. Baldwin. 1927. *Kropotkin's Revolutionary Pamphlets.* London: Vanguard Press, INC.

Roudart, Fadia Panosetti and Laurence. 2022. Evolving Regimes of Land Use and Property in the West Bank Dispossession, Resistance, and Neoliberalism. *Jerusalem Quarterly.*

Salahi, Amr. 2024. *Gaza: What are the Village Leagues Israel plans to replace Hamas?* March 6. http://bit.ly/3FS7N0V

Scott, James C. 1990. *Domination and the Arts of Resistance.* New Haven: Yale University Press.

—. 1976. *The Moral Economy of the Peasant.* New Haven: Yale University Press.

—. 1985. *Weapons of the Weak: Everyday Forms of Peasant Resistance.* New Haven: Yale University Press.

Shahin. n.d. *Nietzsche and Anarchy.* Aragorn Moser.

Shlaim, Avi. 1994. The Oslo Accord. *Journal of Palestine Studies* 24-40.

Shohat, Ella. 2018. The Specter of the Blackamoor. *The University of North Carolina Press* 158-188.

Silva, Eduardo. 2015. Social Movements, Protest, and Policy. *European Review of Latin American and Caribbean Studies* 27-39.

Staggenborg, Aldon Morris and Suzanne. 2002. *Leadership in Social Movements.*

n.d. *Strangeness.* https://dictionary.cambridge.org/dictionary/english/strangeness.

Tartir, Marwa Fatafta and Alaa. 2020. Why Palestinians Need to Reclaim the PLO. *Foreign Policy.* August 20. http://bit.ly/4ei7uJt/.

Team, MBNM. 2024. *Palestine Economic Update May 2024 Middle East Business.* May. http://bit.ly/4jWleuM.

2014. *UN chief welcomes formation of Palestinian unity government.* June 3. http://bit.ly/4jWlk5C.

Žižek, Slavoj. 2023. *The Real Dividing Line in Israel-Palestine Project Syndicate.* October 13. http://bit.ly/45urfv8.

—. 1989. *The Sublime Object of Ideology.* London: VERSO.

Ibraheem Rasras is a PhD student (Political Science & International Relations) at Near East University (Cyprus) and MSc Student (Mediterranean Cooperation and Security) at LUISS University (Italy). He is interested in sociology, modern political economy, and social psychology. He finished his first MA in Human Rights at Doha Institute for Graduate Studies in 2022 and his BA in Human Rights and International Law at Al-Quds Bard College, Palestine (2019). His MA thesis was titled *The Failure of Human Rights System in the Arab Statehood Project: Iraq as a Case Study*. His Ph.D. dissertation is titled *African, De-colonial and Marxist Critiques of the Liberal Values of Human Rights: Zimbabwe as a Case Study*. He has published several articles and essays in different fields, including critical theory, sociology, political science, and international relations.

EU Safety Information

Publisher: Daraja Press, PO BOX 99900 BM 735 664 Wakefield, QC J0X 0C2, Canada

info@darajapress.com | https://darajapress.com

EU Authorized GPSR Representative: Easy Access System Europe – Mustamäe tee 50, 10621 Tallinn, Estonia, gpsr.requests@easproject.com

For EU product safety concerns, please contact us at info@darajapress.com